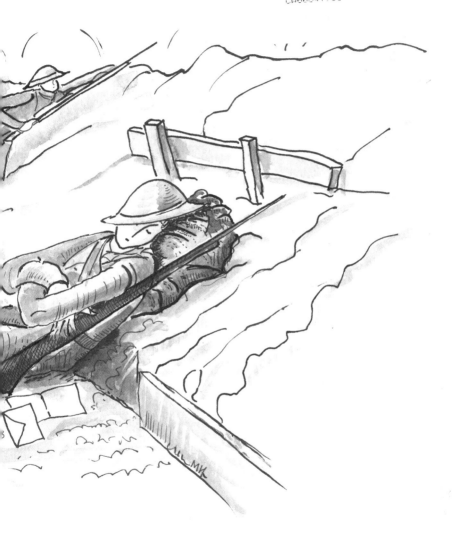

A MILITARY MISCELLANY

A MILITARY MISCELLANY

The combined wit and wisdom of the armed forces

JEREMY ARCHER

Illustrated by Matilda Hunt

To the memory of my father, General Sir John Archer

Illustration on endpapers accompanies Sir George Sitwell's
advice to his son, Osbert, on page 57: 'I find a nap in
the afternoon most helpful, if not unduly prolonged, and
I advise you to try it wherever possible.'

First published 2013
by Elliott and Thompson Limited
27 John Street
London WC1N 2BX
www.eandtbooks.com

ISBN: 978-1-90965-334-4

Text © Jeremy Archer 2013
Illustrations © Matilda Hunt

9 8 7 6 5 4 3 2 1

A CIP catalogue record for this book is available from the British Library.

Typeset by Marie Doherty
Printed in the UK by TJ International

Contents

Foreword

Only somebody with profound expertise in British regimental history, an eye for entertaining detail and a quirky sense of humour would think of producing such a unique compendium of military expressions, habits, songs, dits and traditions. Jeremy Archer has done so painstakingly and to good effect in this compact, well-researched, informative and humorous *Military Miscellany*.

In charting military and naval humour some of the language here is inevitably rather earthy. Indeed, I suspect much of the patter from the drill square and the stories in this book were never really intended to be committed to print. But this compilation pulls those tricks admirably, providing a window on a world that only those who have undergone military training can have experienced for real.

The links to Empire caught my attention in particular; how many of us use Army or Navy *patois* without understanding its origins? There is something to intrigue and amuse everybody in this pithy work, which is also an excellent reference piece.

Peter Wall

General Sir Peter Wall GCB CBE ADC Gen
Chief of the General Staff

Introduction

This little book is exactly what it says it is on the cover: a miscellany. Apart from the Armed Services, there is no theme. If there was a litmus test for inclusion, it is that the reader might perhaps exclaim: 'Oh! that's interesting, I must try to remember that.'

At the back of my mind was a broad intention to try to inform, educate and entertain. With those thoughts in mind, there is a mixture of historical background – interleaved with pathos and poignancy – hopefully leavened with doses of good humour.

Much of the material is derived either from my relatively short experience of service with three British Army infantry regiments – The Devonshire and Dorset Regiment, The Royal Hampshire Regiment and The Worcestershire and Sherwood Foresters Regiment – or from knowledge gained from my research as a published military historian.

By way of discipline, I have deliberately edited down two chapters and two sections – Prayers; Music and Songs; Terms of Endearment and Expressions – otherwise the fun and focus might easily be lost.

Language and Lore

Those who have served would doubtless agree that military service is much more than a job; it is a way of life. As generation has succeeded generation, the language, culture, customs, standards and sense of belonging have developed in subtle – and unsubtle – ways, particularly when the survival of the Nation was in doubt. The funeral of Baroness Thatcher, which took place in St Paul's Cathedral on Wednesday, 17 April 2013, provides a fine example of connection, continuity and a sense of belonging: Garrison Sergeant-Major Bill Mott, Welsh Guards, was the conducting Warrant Officer while his younger brother, Major Nick Mott, Welsh Guards, was the Officer in Charge of the burial party. In the sections that follow I have explored some of these threads.

ACRONYMS

In *Soldiers* (London: HarperPress, 2012), his splendid *tour d'horizon*, published soon after his untimely death, Richard Holmes, for whose support and encouragement over the years I am extremely grateful, wrote that 'adding acronyms stirs that alphabet soup which itself contributes to a military sense of identity by helping form a language all but impenetrable to outsiders'. Having spent ten years in the Army myself, some eminently practical military advice has become hard-wired into my brain, often in the form of acronyms beloved of non-commissioned officer instructors:

KISS 'Keep It Simple, Stupid'

CLAP 'Clearly, Loudly, As an order, with Pauses'

EDI (with particular reference to teaching) 'Explanation, Demonstration, Imitation'

OCD 'Order, Counter-order, Disorder', which, although it has similarities, should not be confused with its contemporary civilian counterpart, Obsessive Compulsive Disorder.

CAKE refers to the British Army's principles of battle procedure:

    C Concurrent activity
    A Anticipation at all levels
    K Knowledge of the grouping system
    E Efficient drills for the receipt and issue of orders

Before his brave Zulu warriors crossed the White Umfolozi River on 17 January 1879, King Cetshwayo's instructions were: 'March slowly, attack at dawn and eat up the red soldiers.' This philosophy can be distilled into a rather more simplified and direct form of **CAKE**: 'Chase, Attack, Kill, Eat'.

This may go some way towards explaining why the Zulu impis triumphed at the Battle of Isandlwana on 22 January 1879, as the British Army's cake rapidly turned to crumbs.

Next come the **Seven Ps**, which must not be confused with T. E. Lawrence's *Seven Pillars of Wisdom*: 'Proper Planning and Preparation Prevents Piss Poor Performance'.

Since examples are always useful – and help imprint such things on the consciousness – I have chosen the Battle of Spion Kop, fought on 23/24 January 1900 between the Ladysmith relief force, commanded by General Sir Redvers Buller, and the Boers besieging Ladysmith, under the command of General Louis Botha. Buller delegated responsibility for the seizure of Spion Kop, a commanding feature in the centre of the Boer line, to Lieutenant General Sir Charles Warren, who had rejoined the Army ten years earlier, after failing to apprehend 'Jack the Ripper' when he was Commissioner of the Metropolitan Police.

A commendably bold and original plan of attack on Spion Kop – later described by John Atkins, *Manchester Guardian* correspondent, as 'that acre of massacre, that complete shambles' – failed disastrously, after a series of seven almost unbelievable omissions and errors on the planning and preparation front:

* Although it is a well-worn military maxim that 'time spent in reconnaissance is seldom wasted', there had been no reconnaissance, either of the approach routes or of the summit itself, beyond that carried out by Lieutenant Colonel

Alexander Thorneycroft, through his telescope. No scouts or patrols had penetrated the defences or established the best approach routes for a night march and assault, that most difficult of military operations.

* While artillery was viewed as a key weapon by both sides, 4th Mountain Battery, stationed some way behind the British front line, never received the order to accompany the assault group, as had been intended.

* As the column of some 2,000 men embarked in the dark on their precipitous climb to the summit of Spion Kop, no one remembered to order the soldiers to pick up a sandbag each, although sufficient sandbags had been made available.

* Just twenty picks and twenty shovels, carried up in stretchers by the Royal Engineers, were available to dig trenches for the assault group. Thirty years earlier, Sir Garnet Wolseley had written that '*The Regimental Entrenching Tools* to accompany a battalion of infantry in the field are as follows: one hundred shovels, 10 spades, 60 pickaxes, 16 felling axes, 2 four-feet and 2 five-feet crowbars. These will be packed in one light waggon, and officers commanding battalions will be held responsible for their safety.'

* Although the battle was fought under the harsh glare of the African sun, the soldiers carried just one water-bottle and one day's field rations each. The officers later searched desperately for the section of water carriers in the darkness – but they were nowhere to be found.

* The trenches were sited in the middle of Spion Kop, rather than on the forward slope, or on the rear of the feature, as the tactics manual recommended. The result was that the

British were unable to cover the dead ground, up which the Boers advanced, while being vulnerable to enfilade fire, from either flank.

★ There was a catastrophic breakdown of communications, to the extent that, after the column commander, Major General Sir Edward Woodgate, had been mortally wounded by shell-fire, no one was quite certain who was in command on the summit of Spion Kop itself. In the darkness and confusion, no oil could be found for the signalling lamp – and so the British withdrew, as the Boers had already done – leaving the latter to reoccupy the peak the following morning.

Two hundred and forty-three British officers and men died within that 'acre of massacre' and their bodies still lie in the pathetically inadequate and ill-sited main British trench. The majority of the British troops who fought – and died – on Spion Kop were from the Lancashire Brigade. Although Woolwich Arsenal's Manor Ground was first referred to as 'the Kop' in 1904, the new open-air embankment at Anfield, home of Liverpool Football Club, was given that name two years later – and still proudly bears it today.

The Defence of Duffer's Drift (London: William Clowes, 1904) by Captain Ernest Dunlop Swinton, Royal Engineers, was first published in the *United Service Magazine* in 1903, less than four years after the Battle of Spion Kop. A notably innovative thinker, Major General Sir Ernest Swinton, as he became, deserves much of the credit for the development and adoption of the tank during the First World War. Among other things, he wrote the first tactical doctrine for armoured warfare. *The Defence of Duffer's Drift* is a highly informative and educational stage-by-stage analysis of how a subaltern's defensive measures gradually evolve, through his experiences in six unsettling dreams. It echoes the wise words of Sir Garnet Wolseley, who wrote in *The Soldier's Pocket-Book for Field Service* (1869): 'Tactical instructions should begin with the company officers learning to handle their fifty or one hundred men as an independent body without supports, when called upon to perform some of the very minor operations of war.'

In 1949, Field Marshal Earl Wavell, himself a veteran of the Second Anglo-Boer War 1899–1902, wrote a foreword to a new edition: 'If the up-to-date young officer asks scornfully what he can possibly learn from the tactics of the Boer War nearly fifty years ago, I can only advise him to read and then inwardly digest some admirable precepts of common sense … If after studying this little work, an officer decides that he has learned nothing, I can only recommend him to apply for employment in an Administrative branch of the War Office; for he will certainly be a danger to troops in the field.' I gave a copy to my brother, as he embarked for the First Gulf War, as a Staff Captain with 7th Armoured Brigade, the 'Desert Rats'.

Then there are the **Seven Ss**, all of which relate to camouflage and the things that a sniper, for example, should think about, in order to avoid giving away his position:

Shape; Shine; Shadow; Silhouette; Spacing; Skyline; Sudden movement

I was amused recently, while attending a seminar on 'chalk stream trout tactics', that the speaker, who had served with the Royal Engineers and the Royal Marines, used the same acronym to remind his audience how best to approach their prey.

There are also, thankfully, acronyms of the more humorous variety: in *On the Psychology of Military Incompetence* (London: Jonathan Cape, 1976), Norman Dixon rather primly describes his 'directly instinctual' human activities – **FFR** – as 'Feeding, Fighting and Reproduction'. When I was serving, FFR meant either transport which was 'fitted for radio', or which was deemed 'fit for role'. In Norman Dixon's example, it was the 'R' that caused all the problems.

While the VC is one of the rarest and is certainly the most highly regarded gallantry award of all, VD (venereal disease) was much more common – and caused real problems in both world wars. Penicillin was first widely used during Operation Husky, the invasion of Sicily, which commenced on the night of 9/10 July 1943. On 29 August 1943, the War Production Board granted nine pharmaceutical companies a licence to manufacture penicillin and, with the ratio of sick to wounded running at an unacceptable ratio of almost three to one during the Italian Campaign, its use was soon sanctioned for the treatment of VD. According to the history of the Royal Army Medical Corps, 'the wastage in men was greatly reduced'. Three years earlier, prior to Dunkirk, Major General (later Field Marshal Viscount) Bernard Montgomery had issued an order concerning how to prevent VD amongst British soldiers, which prompted a marvellous piece of doggerel, written by 'Cupid', who was serving with the Royal Corps of Signals:

Mars Amatoria

The General was worried and was very ill at ease,
He was haunted by the subject of venereal disease;
For four and forty soldiers was the tale he had to tell
Had lain among the beets and loved not wisely but too well.

It was plain that copulation was a tonic for the bored,
  But the gallant British Soldier was an Innocent Abroad;
So 'ere he takes his pleasure with an amateur or whore,
  He must learn the way from officers who've trod that
      path before.
No kind of doubt existed in the Major General's head
  That the men who really knew the game of Love from A to Z
Were his Colonels and his Adjutants and those above the ruck,
  For the higher up an officer the better he can f—k.
The Colonels and the Majors were not a bit dismayed,
  They gave orders for the building of a Unit Love Parade,
And the Adjutants by numbers showed exactly how it's done,
  How not to be a casualty and still have lots of fun.
The Adjutants explained that 'capote' did not mean a cup,
  That refreshment horizontal must be taken standing up,
They told the troops to work at Love according to the rules
  And after digging in to take precautions with their tools.
Now the General is happy and perfectly at ease,
  No longer is he troubled with venereal disease,
His problem solved, his soldiers clean (their badge is
      now a dove),
  He has earned the cross of Venus, our General of Love.

It is unsurprising that the authorities held strong views on 'directly instinctual' human activities in Nazi Germany. For women, it was the **Three Ks**: *Kinder, Küche und Kirche* (children, kitchen and church). To that end, membership of the Bund Deutscher Mädel, or the League of German Maidens, became compulsory on 1 December 1936. The National Socialist Women's League, or NS-Frauenschaft, which espoused these views, was the women's wing of the Nazi Party.

❖

In military parlance, **SITREP** stands for Situation Report. 'Send SITREP, over,' was regularly heard on British Army radio networks. During the Second World War, US servicemen and -women introduced a completely different – and rather refreshing – take on SITREPs. In order of increasing seriousness, here is a selection of US SITREPs:

SNAFU   Situation Normal; All Fucked Up
SUSFU   Situation Unchanged; Still Fucked Up
FUMTU   Fucked Up More Than Usual
TARFU   Things Are Really Fucked Up
FUBAR   Fucked Up Beyond All Recognition

In the British Army, the code name 'mushroom' means a watch-keeper in one of the many headquarters, whose job it is to monitor, transcribe and facilitate traffic on the radio networks. In the trade, mushrooms are invariably known – not entirely inaccurately – as **KIDFOS** or 'Kept In the Dark and Fed On Shit'.

This reminds me of a rather good story, which underlines just how tedious life could be for a KIDFOS. In the autumn of 1983, I was the Regimental Signals Officer of the 1st Battalion, The Worcestershire and Sherwood Foresters Regiment, but had been loaned to Brigade Headquarters as a watch-keeper for Exercise Eternal Triangle, the final divisional exercise of the year. We were on radio silence, which meant that there was absolutely nothing to listen to anyway. Whenever a transmission was made, the Clansman radio 'pressel switch' was depressed and there was a squelchy sound. We heard that noise, just before a soft voice said: 'Are there any other friendly teddy bears out there?' Fifteen minutes later, it happened again: 'Are there really no friendly bears out there?' Provoked beyond endurance, the Divisional Commander snapped back: 'Hello all stations, this is zero, we are on radio silence – repeat, radio silence – out.' After a respectable interval, the first, now rather plaintive, voice said: 'You're not a very friendly teddy bear, are you?' The whole company of KIDFOSes fell about laughing – and the culprit was never identified.

My introduction to cavalry radio procedure came during a battle group exercise on Soltau Training Area in northern Germany, written and controlled by The 5th Royal (Inniskilling) Dragoon Guards, otherwise known as 'the Skins'. It was an advance to contact by armour and mechanised infantry. On the operations map, there was a series of report lines, the code names of which were given over the battle group radio net when each line had been successfully consolidated. In order to make things more fun – and perhaps provide greater incentive to the participants – the report lines had been arranged in a suitably seductive manner: 'stilettos', 'stockings', 'garters', 'skirt', 'blouse', 'brassiere', 'panties' – before we finally reached the objective. Even the Cold War had its hotter moments!

Maps, such as those in the previous tale, were frequently protected with something called 'talc', on which one could then write, using Chinagraph pencils. It has only recently been pointed out to me that, in typical Army fashion, **TALC** stands for 'Training Aid, Linoleum, Clear'. I always wondered – but never had the courage to ask.

Although unrelated to acronyms, it seems a pity not to include two enduring memories of an Op Banner tour in Northern Ireland in early 1979. One of my section commanders was Corporal 'Yogi' Johnson, the origin of whose nickname is lost in the mists of time, although he certainly was a bit of a joker, like Yogi Bear. We were stationed in the old Grand Central Hotel, Belfast, a much-bombed building which the British Army had first taken over in 1972. 'Yogi' Johnson had two notices pinned to the walls of his shared room. One read 'Be Alert: the Army needs Lerts'; the other read 'When on patrol, don't walk, boogie'. With that attitude and sense of humour, a four-month operational tour flies past surprisingly quickly. In the mid-1980s the Grand Central Hotel was demolished to make way for Westfield CastleCourt shopping centre.

One of the most testing phases of warfare is that which takes place in villages, towns and cities, where obstacles and cover work to the defenders' advantage. This was known as **FIBUA**, or 'Fighting In a Built-Up Area'. Soldiers often refer to it, irreverently, as **FISH & CHIPS** or 'Fighting In Someone's House and Creating Havoc in Public Spaces'.

NAAFI stands for the 'Navy, Army and Air Force Institutes', which was founded in 1921 to run recreational establishments for the British Armed Forces and to sell goods to servicemen and -women and their families. Inevitably, over the years, it has acquired some irreverent nicknames, including 'Never 'Ave Any Fags In', 'Not Anywhere Around the Falkland Islands' and 'No Ambition And Fuck-all Interest'. On 23 January 1959, *The Spectator* published a rather splendid clerihew:

> *The NAAFI*
> *Is a sort of caafi*
> *Where soldiers are rude*
> *About the food.*

Thinking of food, the verb scoff – meaning to eat greedily – has an interesting derivation. Having always thought that it had its origins in the nineteenth-century French chef, Auguste Escoffier, who worked at the Savoy Hotel, I was interested to read that it comes from the Dutch, *schoft*, which evolved into the Cape Dutch, *schoff*, meaning a quarter of a day, or time for a meal, and was first used during the Second Anglo-Boer War. Wherever the truth lies, I much prefer to believe that we use it in honour of **SCOFF** – or 'Senior Catering Officer Field Force' – responsible for making such arrangements. Strong supporting evidence for this theory is that scoff was first included as an intransitive verb in the *Oxford English Dictionary* in 1899, the year war was declared. Nor were the animals ignored during that campaign: the roads of South Africa are lined with wide banks of cosmos, an alien species brought into the country in the British Army's horse-feed, which was sourced from Mexico. Not all horses were so lucky, though. With rations running low in besieged Ladysmith, Major Cecil Park, The Devonshire Regiment, wrote: 'The new horse soup, known as "Chevril," is most excellent stuff, and tastes like best beef-tea.' The name Chevril was a variation on the popular beef extract, Bovril. Park continued: 'Some of the men won't touch it, simply because they know it is horse, silly idiots; but the majority like it and clamour for more.'

Pilots frequently have a rather high opinion of themselves, which may have something to do with the rarefied atmosphere in which they work. Army pilots are often referred to as **GIGJAM**s or 'God I'm Good: Just Ask Me'. I wish I had known this a little earlier, since I could have had an enjoyable discussion with my late father-in-law, Major General David Goodman, who served as Director, Army Air Corps from 1983 to 1987. Something that he certainly would not have disagreed with, though, was **QNPBT** or 'Quick Nervous Peek Before Take-off', which seems only sensible as a pre-flight drill.

Common in civilian – particularly office – life as well, **BOGSAT** might be describing a bodily function. In fact, it refers to a 'Bunch Of Guys Sitting Around Talking'. In the context of Afghanistan and the Pashtun people, this probably describes a *loya jirga* – or local 'grand council' – pretty accurately. Somehow, if one attempts to be politically correct and gender-inclusive, **BOPSAT** does not have quite the same ring about it.

During the Second World War, in order to ensure that fuel was quickly and efficiently made available after the invasion of Normandy, two pipe-lines were laid under the English Channel. One went from Shanklin on the Isle of Wight to Cherbourg and the other from Dungeness to Boulogne. These were named **PLUTO** – which stands, ever-so-slightly inaccurately, for 'Pipe Line Under The Ocean' – after Mickey Mouse's pet dog, which appeared in no fewer than eighty-nine short Walt Disney films between 1930 and 1953.

The name, Fido, which means 'I am faithful', was first popularised for dogs by Abraham Lincoln. The British Army's usage is altogether more brutal: in case of an incident that might well lead to an unacceptable delay, **FIDO** over the radio net means, very simply and succinctly, 'Fuck It! Drive On!' There was at least one Royal Navy precedent. As the Allied invasion fleet sailed across the Channel in deteriorating weather conditions on the night of 5 June 1944, Rear Admiral A. G. Talbot, who was in charge of amphibious operations off Sword Beach, flew the signal: 'Good luck, drive on.'

Military headquarters, of whatever level, regularly take officers and senior ranks aside for training sessions in the field. Since there was no involvement from the soldiery, these were referred to as a **TEWT** or a 'Tactical Exercise Without Troops'. To unwilling attendees, they were known as a 'Pointless Exercise Not Involving Soldiers'. Work it out! The cynics soon devised similar schemes, such as a **PEWC**: a 'Parking Exercise Without Cars'; or perhaps a **JEWT**: a 'Jungle Exercise Without Trees'; or even a **NEWD**: a 'Night Exercise Without Darkness'. The Royal Army Chaplains' Department, widely known as either the 'Sky Pilots' or as the 'God Botherers', was far from immune: in their case, a **PEWC** was known as a 'Padre's Exercise Without Congregation', while a **BEWB** was a 'Burial Exercise Without Body'. The end of every exercise was always announced by a single word, 'ENDEX' over the radio net. In practice, we preferred to use the much more expressive term, **PUFO**, or 'Pack Up! Fuck Off!'

For a variety of reasons, there has always been some tension between the Regular Army and the Territorial – or so-called weekend – Army. At its worst, this manifested itself in a couple of slightly unpleasant and unnecessary acronyms: a **STAB** was a 'Stupid Territorial Army Bastard', while an **ARAB** was an 'Arrogant Regular Army Bastard'.

Bearing in mind that it is always important to know to whom you are talking – and where they fit into the organisation – one can occasionally be tempted to make use of the disparaging acronym, **PONI**, or 'Person Of No Importance'. In the same way, both officers and soldiers resented those promoted, along the lines of the Peter Principle, to their level of incompetence. Members of one stratum were widely known as **GOPWO**s, or 'Grossly Over-Promoted Warrant Officers'.

While the British Army affectionately refers to young recruits as **CROW**s – from Combat Recruit Of War – the US Army has its **GI**s. G.I. was originally the abbreviation for galvanized iron, routinely recorded in that way in inventories. During the First World War, though, G.I. began to mean Government Issue. Just two decades later, a G.I. was an enlisted man, with the term 'G.I. Joe' being popularised by David Breger's cartoon strip of the same name, which appeared in the first issue of *Yank, The Army Weekly* on 17 June 1942.

In a fitness-obsessed world, officers sometimes get things badly wrong. In military terms, **ORBAT** stands for Order of Battle. There is, though, an alternative meaning, which is a touch cruel to all ranks. An officer who spends too much time in the gym, toning his or her lats, pecs and triceps, might perhaps end up with an **ORBAT**: an Other Rank's Body And Torso.

Finally, there is a thought-provoking acronym. Bearing in mind the hugely depressing statistic that more than 20 per cent of the homeless in London have Service connections, there is a significant safety net, comprising a broad range of Service charities, all performing subtly different roles, having taken into account a range of factors, grouped under the mnemonic, **HERBS**:

H Health, emotional and physical
E Environment, situation and condition
R Resources, financial, home care and travel
B Background service, mobility, previous assistance
S Social relations, family support, separation/bereavement

Those interested in further reading may wish to check out the **AR**my **R**umour **SE**rvice (ARRSE): www.arrse.co.uk.

TERMS OF ENDEARMENT

During my military service, I have happy memories of seeing envelopes – both incoming and outward-bound – covered with apparently meaningless letter groupings. Many years later, I found one such letter, which had somehow become folded into my map-case – and for which the poor lad is presumably still waiting patiently. It took a while for me to realise that this was a continuation of a Second World War tradition, which happily sanctioned affectionate love tokens such as:

SWALK   Sealed With A Loving Kiss
ITALY   I Trust And Love You
WALES   With All Love Eternal Sweetheart
BELFAST   Be Ever Loving Faithful And Stay True
HOLLAND   Hope Our Love Lasts And Never Dies
FRANCE   Friendship Remains And Never Can End

Over time, these became far more suggestive and racy so, after six of one, here are half-a-dozen of the other, offering a range of adventurous destinations:

NORWICH   (K)Nickers Off Ready When I Come Home
CHINA   Come Home I Need Action
MALAYA   My Ardent Lips Await Your Arrival
USSR   Under Sofa Stripped (and) Ready
BURMA   Be Undressed (and) Ready My Angel
EGYPT   Eager (to) Grab Your Pretty Tits

To make such a public display of affection must have demanded a measure of **GUTS**, which is altogether more forceful: 'Get Up Them Stairs'.

My personal favourite – which makes no sense at all as an acronym, unless it is an obscure Welsh railway station or a Second World War Russian bomber – has a charm all of its own:

ILYTTDFOATCCSH   I Love You Till The Deserts Freeze Over And The Camels Come Skating Home

❖

Sadly, there was too often another side to such communications: these are the so-called 'Dear John' letters, bringing relationships to an end. On 17 August 1945, just two days after the ceasefire with Japan at the end of the Second World War, the *Democrat and Chronicle*, a newspaper based in Rochester, New York State, wrote: '"Dear John", the letter began. "I have found someone else whom I think the world of. I think the only way out is for us to get a divorce," it said. They usually begin like that, those letters that told of infidelity on the part of the wives of servicemen.'

When I was serving in Germany in the late 1970s, there was said to be a not-so-secret code at work on 'the patch', where officers and soldiers lived in married quarters. Lever Brothers, now Unilever, launched its OMO laundry detergent brand as long ago as 1954. Apparently, a packet of OMO positioned subtly – or not so subtly – on the windowsill indicated either 'On My Own', or 'Old Man's Out', which amounts to the same thing. Against that backdrop, it is scarcely credible that the advertising strap-lines associated with the brand over the years include 'Dirt is good', 'Multiactive', 'Active fresh', 'Front loader; Small and mighty capsules', 'Progress', 'Ultimate' and 'Sensitive'. Although no longer sold in the United Kingdom, OMO is still available in Germany – apparently.

Another, rather vulgar, acronym draws together the threads of social interaction in the British Army of the Rhine (BAOR) in Cold War-dominated West Germany. As rehearsed time and time again, 4 Division's key role was to delay the Eastern Bloc armies in the so-called Sibbesse Gap – defined as 'ground of tactical importance' – thus buying time to enable the rest of BAOR to redeploy further back, in prepared positions. Life in

BAOR could become a little tedious and repetitive and when all that pent-up enthusiasm for partying was finally released, as well as being the national flag-carrier, **LUFTHANSA** in those far-off days stood for 'Let's Fuck The Hostess And Not Say Anything'!

NICKNAMES

In its issue of 12 April 1740 the magazine, *The Craftsman*, recorded a 'Conversation between Thomas Lobster, soldier, and John Tar, sailor'. Since they wore red coats, soldiers were known as 'lobsters', while, dressed in blue, sailors were referred to as 'blue bottles'. In 1843, when the *Soldier's Pocket Book* was first introduced, the sample name for correct completion, Thomas Atkins – later immortalised by Rudyard Kipling in his poem of 1892 – was chosen by the Duke of Wellington, in memory of a steadfast soldier with whom he had served in the 33rd (Duke of Wellington's) Regiment of Foot.

The subject of regimental nicknames has been so well trawled over in the past, even forming the subject of a book by Tim Carew (*How the Regiments Got Their Nicknames*, Barnsley: Leo Cooper, 1975), who once served with The Devonshire Regiment, that there seems little point in covering all the same ground again. What I have decided to do, therefore, is use my own regiment to illustrate the three most common ways in which nicknames came about: distinction in the field; colour variation in the uniform; and behaviour that did not necessarily commend itself to Horse Guards, the Headquarters of the British Army.

The Devonshire and Dorset Regiment was the result of the amalgamation of The Devonshire Regiment and The Dorset

Regiment, which took place on 17 May 1958. Until 1782, in which year colonels were invited to propose appropriate county designations, a regiment was referred to using the surname of its colonel. Prior to the Childers Reforms of 1881, the first twenty-five regiments of foot each had two battalions while, with just two exceptions, the remaining 109 were single battalion regiments. Thus, while the 11th (North Devonshire) Regiment of Foot remained unaffected by the 1881 reforms – beyond dropping the 'North' – the 39th (Dorsetshire) and the 54th (West Norfolk) Regiments of Foot were amalgamated to form the 1st and 2nd Battalions, the Dorsetshire Regiment respectively. There was no particular logic behind such combinations. According to the *Historical Record of the 39th Foot* (London: 1853): 'On the 29th of October 1807, His Majesty King George III was pleased to direct that the county title of the Thirty-Ninth regiment should be changed from East Middlesex to Dorsetshire', which had been borne hitherto by the 35th Regiment of Foot.

Following the Battle of Salamanca on 22 July 1812, during which the 11th Regiment of Foot distinguished itself, suffering 340 casualties out of a strength of 516 officers and men present that day, the regiment acquired the hard-earned nickname, 'the Bloody Eleventh'.

While regiments of the line all wore knee-length red coats, with deep cuffs and broad lapels, they were distinguished by their facings and linings, which could be clearly seen when the 'skirts' were hooked back in order to free legs for marching. The 39th Regiment of Foot, which was raised in 1702, wore green facings and linings, from which their nickname, 'the Green Linnets', naturally followed. In 1744 two regiments had colonels called Howard, but one regiment wore green facings while the other had buff-coloured facings. The 19th Regiment of Foot, whose colonel was the Hon. Sir Charles Howard, was called the 'Green Howards', while the 3rd Regiment of Foot, whose colonel was Lieutenant General Thomas Howard, was referred to as 'Howard's Buffs'.

The 54th Regiment of Foot, which was raised in 1755, first saw serious active service during the American War of Independence. Led by the traitor, Benedict Arnold, they took part in the final, successful offensive undertaken by the British garrison of New York, against a troublesome privateer base at New London, Connecticut. On 6 September 1781, the 54th landed on the eastern side of the estuary of the Thames River and stormed Fort Griswold, before setting fire to a dozen vessels, laden with stores and merchandise. The fire spread to the town itself, which was largely destroyed, leading to the 54th's nickname, 'the Flamers'.

On 21 June 1813, as the Battle of Vitoria drew to a close, an exhausted but exhilarated British Army turned its attention – neither for the first, nor the last, time – to pillage, rather than pursuit. The 14th Light Dragoons intercepted the baggage train of Joseph Bonaparte, King José I of Spain, elder brother of Napoleon Bonaparte, acquiring in the process his silver chamberpot. While the captive liquid has changed – and this precious object now holds the champagne served at Guest Nights in the Officers' Mess of The King's Royal Hussars – the regiment had earned itself the proud nickname, 'the Emperor's Chambermaids'.

During the early nineteenth century, the Rothschild family steadily acquired estates in Buckinghamshire and Hertfordshire, including Ascott House, Mentmore Towers, Waddesdon Manor and Tring Park. The close interest that the family took in The Royal Buckinghamshire Hussars led to the regiment being known as 'the Flying Foreskins'.

The five battalions of The Royal Fusiliers, which together comprised the Jewish Legion, were known as 'the Judeans', of which nickname they and their community were justly proud. Formed in Plymouth in January 1918, the 38th, 39th and 40th (Service) Battalions saw service, appropriately enough, in the Middle East, while the 41st and 42nd Battalions remained in England and provided conscripts. When the battalions were disbanded in 1919, many of the soldiers settled in the Holy Land. Lieutenant Colonel J. H. Patterson told their story in his book, *With the Judeans in the Palestine Campaign*, published by Macmillan (New York) in 1922. The Jewish Legion was also known as 'the New Maccabeans', 'the Royal Jewsiliers' and 'the King's Own Schneiders'. Fortunately, it was much more typical of British soldiers' sense of humour that they were more commonly referred to as 'the Jordan Highlanders'.

The supporting elements of the British Army were far from immune from that sense of humour. The Army Hospital Corps was wittily known as 'the Linseed Lancers'. After becoming the Royal Army Medical Corps, they were sometimes known, most unkindly, as 'Rob All My Comrades', on the basis that they routinely rifled casualties' pockets. In a class-conscious pre-war British Army, they were also known as 'Rather A Mixed Crowd'; however, it was worse for the IMS, the Indian Medical Service, who were apparently 'Infinitely More So'.

In a similar vein, the Army Service Corps was known as 'Ally Sloper's Cavalry', after a comic strip character, drawn by W. F. Thomas, who had the habit of 'sloping off down the alley' when the rent collector called. After becoming the Royal

Army Service Corps in 1918, they were occasionally known, equally unfairly, as 'Run Away, Someone's Coming'. The Royal Army Ordnance Corps were known – descriptively, rather than pejoratively – as the 'Rag And Oil Company'.

Two regiments acquired nicknames based purely on the shape and order of their numbers, without a hint of sexual connotation. The 69th (South Lincolnshire) Regiment of Foot, later the 2nd Battalion, The Welsh Regiment, was known as 'the Ups and Downs'; while the 96th Regiment of Foot, later the 2nd Battalion, The Manchester Regiment, was called 'the Bendovers'.

Indian words were both a puzzle and a pleasure to British servicemen, with the result that a number of Indian Army regiments acquired playful nicknames. The 9th Bhopal Infantry was known as the 'Bo Peeps', while the Rajputana Rifles was called – presumably not to their face – the 'Large Banana Trifles'.

SERGEANT-MAJORS' CRIES

The first five weeks at the Royal Military Academy Sandhurst are largely – but by no means entirely – taken up with drill, with the ultimate goal of 'passing off the square'. Historically, the rationale behind drill movements was clear and logical: to inculcate instinctive obedience to the word of command; to enable bodies of men to be manoeuvred around the battlefield, in ways most suited to the terrain and also to the enemy's formations; to instil confidence in nervous soldiers by issuing orders with which they were totally familiar, so that the responses became instinctive; and to mould a body of men together, to the extent that no one wanted to let his mates down.

The Royal Military Academy Sandhurst focuses on the final point, with a series of sergeant-majors' parade ground cries helping recalcitrant officer cadets on their way. The first task is to explain the nature of the relationship:

* 'Gentlemen, you call me Sir, and I call you Sir, the difference is that you will mean it – while I don't yet, Sir.'

* 'Gentlemen, when I speak to you, I will begin and end with Sir – but I can make no assurances whatsoever about what comes in between.'

Then the drill begins, with ritual humiliation often the order of the day:

* 'Sir, you march as if you are suffering from the biggest dose of haemorrhoids in the world, Sir.'

* 'Sir, you're marching like Spiderman with an erection, Sir!'

* 'Sir, your shirt looks as if it has escaped from your kitbag and leapt straight on to your back, Sir.'

* 'Sir, you might have broken your mother's heart – but you're certainly not going to break mine, Sir.'

* 'Sir, am I hurting you? I should be because I'm standing on your hair, Sir!'

* 'Gentlemen, stop looking down, get your heads up. There's no money on this square.'

* 'Sir, you're getting everything wrong! Are you on Fullers Earth? Because you're definitely not on this one, Sir.'

* ✱ 'Gentlemen, rip your head and eyes to the front. I want to see eyeballs all over the square!'

* ✱ 'Sir, if you don't stop stepping short, I'll stick this pace-stick where the sun doesn't shine and open it to 30 inches, Sir!'

* ✱ 'Gentlemen, close your mouths and stop catching flies.'

* ✱ 'Sir, stand still or I'll drop-kick you over the NAAFI, Sir.'

* ✱ 'Sir, I am going to buy a packet of Durex and send it to your father to make absolutely sure he doesn't breed another useless ---- like you, Sir.'

* ✱ 'Sir, swing your arms shoulder-high – or I will rip one of them off and beat you to death with the soggy end, Sir.'

* ✱ 'Sir, I want you to imagine that your scabbard had hair round it and then, with a bit of luck, you might actually be able to return your sword, Sir.'

CONFIDENTIAL REPORTS

Britannia Royal Naval College Dartmouth, the Royal Military Academy Sandhurst and the RAF College Cranwell are only the start. Officers' annual Confidential Reports include plenty of witty put-downs and career full stops – apocryphal or otherwise – that resonate down the years. While familiar with many of these, I thought that it was best to quote from an official website, *The Management of Defence*, on www. armedforces.co.uk:

* 'Works well when under constant supervision and cornered like a rat in a trap.'

* 'He has the wisdom of youth, and the energy of old age.'

* 'This officer should go far – and the sooner he starts, the better.'

* 'This officer is depriving a village somewhere of its idiot.'

* 'Only occasionally wets himself under pressure.'

* 'This officer is really not so much of a has-been, but more of a definitely won't-be.'

* 'When she opens her mouth, it seems that this is only to change whichever foot was previously in there.'

* 'He has carried out each and every one of his duties to his entire satisfaction.'

* 'He would be out of his depth in a car park puddle.'

* 'Technically sound, but socially impossible.'

* 'This officer reminds me very much of a gyroscope – always spinning around at a frantic pace, but not really going anywhere.'

* 'This young man has delusions of adequacy.'

* 'When he joined my ship, this officer was something of a granny; since then he has aged considerably.'

* 'This Medical Officer has used my ship to carry his genitals from port to port, and my officers to carry him from bar to bar.'

* 'Since my last report he has reached rock bottom, and has started to dig.'

* 'She sets low personal standards and then consistently fails to achieve them.'

* 'His men would follow him anywhere, but only out of curiosity.'

* 'I would not breed from this officer.'

* 'This officer has the astonishing ability to provoke something close to a mutiny every time he opens his mouth.'

To this selection, I would like to add two of my own:

* 'This officer consistently pushes doors clearly marked pull.'

★ 'This officer is like a lighthouse in the desert: very, very bright but of absolutely no use to passing shipping.'

ROYAL NAVY SIGNALS

When signals were sent by officers and men of the Royal Navy, the use of succinct quotations from the Bible was considered both subtle and also suitable practice, often enabling the guilty party to escape punishment.

By way of example, Captain (Retired) Stephen Taylor RN explained that, as Captain of HMS *Southampton*, he had once had the misfortune to send Admiral Sir Benjamin Bathurst by helicopter to the Type 22 frigate, HMS *Brazen*, instead of to her sister ship, HMS *London*, since the two were the wrong way round on the plot. The Admiral was late so, by way of apology, Stephen sent the following signal: 'Amos chapter 8 verses 9–10' or, in translation, 'And it shall come to pass in that day, saith the Lord God, that I will cause the sun to go down at noon, and I will darken the earth in the clear day: And I will turn your feasts into mourning, and all your songs into lamentation; and I will bring up sackcloth upon all loins, and baldness upon every head; and I will make it as the mourning of an only son, and the end thereof as a bitter day.'

Such quotations, to suit every occasion, were built up over the years by captains and signals officers. To that end, Stephen told me that 'we always had to have a copy of the Bible in the Wireless Office.' Furthermore, he kindly suggested that I should consult *Make A Signal* by Jack Broome, published by Putnam in 1955, for a few more examples:

* A submarine returning unscathed from a war patrol signalled the flotilla Captain: 'Psalm 17 verse 4' or, in translation, 'Concerning the works of men, by the word of thy lips I have kept me from the paths of the destroyer.'

* After receiving congratulations by signal on his recent promotion, an officer replied: 'VMT. Psalm 140, 2nd half of verse 5' or, in translation, 'They have set gins for me.'

* When HMS *Phoebe* departed one command, in order to join another, the following signal was sent to the new command: 'Romans chapter 16 verses 1 and 2' or, in translation, 'I commend unto you Phebe our sister, which is a servant of the church which is at Cenchrea: That ye receive her in the Lord, as becometh saints, and that ye assist her in whatsoever business she hath need of you: for she hath been a succourer of many, and of myself also.'

* A Royal Navy corvette signalled the Commander-in-Chief, Plymouth: '*Roman Emperor* in tow badly damaged please send tugs'. The reply read: 'Revelations chapter 3 verse 11' or, in translation, 'Behold, I come quickly: hold that fast which thou hast, that no man take thy crown.'

* When a cruiser, commanded by Captain Wright, left the squadron, the following farewell message was sent: 'Proverbs 16 verse 8' or, in translation, 'Better is a little with righteousness than great revenues without right.'

* When he considered that one of his squadrons had failed to obey orders, the Fleet Air Arm Commander in an aircraft carrier signalled: 'This is Master quoting Hebrews chapter 12 verse 8. I quote: But if ye be without chastisement,

whereof all are partakers, then are ye bastards. Unquote. I say again bastards. Out.'

★ After a convoy had emerged from thick fog and merchant ships and their escorts had sorted themselves out, with the result that the noise of sirens slowly faded away, the Escort Commander sent the following general signal: 'Job chapter 42 verse 5', or, in translation, 'I have heard of thee by the hearing of the ear: but now mine eye seeth thee.'

★ The stirring words of William Shakespeare were sometimes invoked. During the winter of 1940, as four destroyers of 5th Flotilla, under the command of Captain Lord Louis Mountbatten in HMS *Kelly*, approached the Atlantic coast of Scotland in dreadful conditions, uncertain of their exact position, HMS *Kipling* sent a signal: 'Attention is invited to The Tempest Act 1 Scene 1 last 4 lines' or, in translation, in the words of Gonzalo, an honest old Counsellor: 'Now would I give a thousand furlongs of sea for an acre of barren ground – long heath, brown furze, any thing. The wills above be done! but I would fain die a dry death.'

★ My personal favourite dates from 4 May 1945, when two British aircraft carriers, HMS *Formidable* and HMS *Indomitable*, the latter flying the flag of Vice Admiral Sir Philip Vian, Flag Officer Commanding, 1st Aircraft Carrier Squadron, were both struck by bomb-laden Kamikaze *Zeros*. After HMS *Indomitable* had been hit, the Captain of HMS *Formidable* signalled: 'Little yellow bastard'. The Admiral signalled back: 'Are you referring to me?'

✶ Target-towing for live-firing practice – whether at sea or in the air – is fraught with danger. With shells exploding rather closer to his aircraft than to the target, one nervous and angry pilot felt obliged to remind a party of Royal Navy anti-aircraft gunners: 'I am pulling this bloody thing, not pushing it.' In a signal that anticipated those often seen above gentlemen's urinals, an irritable tug captain signalled the cruiser for which he was towing a surface target: 'We aim to please. You aim too please.'

Since guests on *Desert Island Discs* are always offered the Bible and a complete edition of Shakespeare, requesting a fully-functional flag signalling system as their luxury could only improve the chances of being rescued.

BUGLE CALLS

The word bugle is derived from the Latin, *buculus*, or young ox. While bugles were traditionally made from the hollowed-out horns of oxen, they are now made from brass or copper, in the form of a tube, wound twice around a small bell. Using bugle calls to pass instructions to troops was first practised by German soldiers in the mid-eighteenth century, when the noise of beating drums, which had been universally used for that purpose hitherto, proved to be too low-pitched to cut through the noise of battle.

There are three components to a bugle call: the prefix, which identifies the company, battalion, brigade or division to which the call applies; the call itself; concluding with the suffix, which specifies those being addressed, the time that it takes effect, or the urgency of the call.

Bugle calls had to be learned – and the best way to do so was to put appropriate words to the call. As a Regimental Signals Officer, I had to learn Morse Code and achieve ten words a minute: it was extra Morse before breakfast every morning until that (rather low) standard was attained. The letter 'Q' is represented by --.- or Dah Dah Dit Dah – which sounds (slightly) like 'Here comes the Queen'. It was only by finding sound associations that I eventually conquered Morse Code. It was the same with bugle calls. Over the years, strings of often irreverent – but never irrelevant – words have become associated with the different bugle calls:

Rouse 'Get out of bed, get out of bed, get out of bed, you lazy devils. Hands off your cocks, put on your socks, get out of the bed, you lazy devils.'

Fall in 'Fall in A, fall in B, fall in every company; fall in A, fall in B, fall in every company.'

Nine o'clock 'Put your clocks right, put your clocks right, put your clocks right by me.'

Picquet 'Come and do a picquet, boys, come and do a guard. You may think it's easy, boys, but it's fucking hard.'

Quarter-hour's dress 'You've got a face like a chicken's arse; you've got a face like a chicken's arse.'

Cookhouse 'Come to the cookhouse door, boys, come to the cookhouse door.'

Sick parade 'Sixty-four, ninety-four, he'll never go sick any more: the poor fellow's dead.' This call has its origins in Army Form 6494, the old-style sick report, which is still used by a number of medical authorities.

Mail   'Letter for me; letter for you. Letter from lousy Lizzie; letter from lousy Lou.'

Officers   'Officers come and be cursed: run, run, run!'

Sergeants   'Tom Tucker, Tom Tucker, you dirty old fucker; Tom Tucker, Tom Tucker, go fuck her!'

Officers' dinner in half-an-hour   'Half-hour's dress to officers' mess; half-hour's dress to officers' mess.'

Officers' dinner   'The Officers' wives make puddings and pies; the Sergeants' wives make skelly; but all the Guardsman ever gets is a great big swank for his belly.'

Pioneer   'Pioneer, pioneer, pioneer, pioneer, there a dog shit on the square, pioneer, pioneer; dog shit shouldn't be there.'

General alarm   'Hang your balls on the walls; hang your balls on the walls; run! run!, run!'

General Salute   'Stand to attention, you red-arsed recruits and don't make a balls of the General Salute.'

EXPRESSIONS

While the size of the British Army has fluctuated wildly over the years – from some 680,000 men at the height of the Napoleonic Wars, to just 91,000 regular soldiers in 1838, to almost half-a-million in uniform during the Second Anglo-Boer War, to a British Expeditionary Force, which numbered some 80,000 in August 1914 but peaked at more than two million – there are a great many expressions that, whether or not the users know their origins, came out of the Royal Navy, the British Army or the Royal Air Force:

'He went bald-headed at it'   he just went for it, the consequences be damned. John Manners, Marquess of Granby, who had turned bald by the age of twenty-four, commanded a cavalry brigade at the Battle of Warburg on 31 July 1760, during the Seven Years' War. According to one observer, he is said to 'have lost his hat and wig, forcing him to salute his commander without them', with the result that non-commissioned officers and troopers of The Blues and Royals are the only soldiers in the British Army who may salute without wearing headdress. Shocked that so many soldiers left the Army with no money and poor prospects, the Marquess of Granby generously arranged for many former soldiers 'of good standing' to receive a gratuity, paid from his own pocket. When he died on 18 October 1770, the Marquess left debts of some £60,000, the equivalent of more than £6,000,000 today. In acknowledgement of their unexpected windfall, many of the soldiers later opened public houses named The Marquess of Granby. The Government subsequently adopted the policy of rewarding long and loyal military service with a gratuity.

'Slipshod'   careless or slovenly. When left to their own devices, young officers tended to dress down and relax, even donning carpet slippers, thus becoming slipshod, at least as far as their superiors were concerned.

'Hand over fist'   steadily and rapidly. As sailors climb the rigging, they ascend 'hand over fist', seizing hold of alternate ratlines; equally, as bankers greedily seize money with one hand, so they reach out to grab more with the other.

'He was swinging the lead'   shirking. Soundings of the depth of water beneath a ship's hull were taken by swinging a line weighted with lead over the side and noting at what mark on the line it went slack. A lazy sailor would take his time over the task, so shirkers are said to be 'swinging the lead'. Samuel Langhorne Clemens worked on the Mississippi riverboats, where the cry, "Mark twain!" – which he later took as his *nom de plume* – indicated a depth of two fathoms, or 'safe water'.

'I heard it straight from the horse's mouth'   so it must be true. Although there are two potential origins of this phrase, I strongly favour the military one. The first derives from the horse-racing world, with the advice of stable lads, trainers and owners being regarded as 'almost as good as hearing it straight from the horse's mouth', since they know their business. The military one refers to Horse Guards, the Headquarters of the British Army from 1722 to 1858: if one has heard something directly from a source at Horse Guards, then it could not possibly be wrong, could it?

'It went off half-cock'   something that did not quite work out as had been expected. When using the old-fashioned musket, the hammer was set at half-cock, which meant that it should not, therefore, have gone off – but sometimes it did. In modern military parlance, this would be referred to as a 'negligent discharge', which is a very serious, chargeable offence.

'It was a flash in the pan'   a disappointing end, after a rather promising beginning. The origin is that, although the striking of the flint resulted in a flash in the musket's priming pan, the main charge failed to ignite and the weapon did not, therefore, discharge, which resulted in it 'hanging fire'.

'Lock, stock and barrel'   everything. The three essential components of an old-fashioned musket or flint-lock are: the lock, which holds the flint back, until the trigger is pressed; the stock, which the user pulls into his shoulder; and the barrel, down which the ball is fired. In his 1891 debut novel, *The Light that Failed*, Rudyard Kipling wrote: 'The whole thing, lock, stock, and barrel, isn't worth one big yellow sea-poppy.'

'Keep your powder dry'   take good care and be prepared for any eventuality. Colonel Valentine Blacker, who had fought the Marathas in India's Deccan from 1817 to 1819, put the following words into the mouth of Oliver Cromwell, as the latter's force was about to cross a river: 'Put your trust in God, boys, and keep your powder dry.'

'Taking down a peg'   putting someone in their place. In Indian military cantonments there was a board above each barrel of rum or arrack (local spirit), on which were written the names of those entitled to a regular issue. Beneath each name there were two holes, one above the other. A peg was placed in the top hole when the first tot, colloquially known as a 'gum-tickler', was issued – and then moved to the bottom hole when that day's ration was complete, with the so-called 'gall-burster'. If someone gave his tot to a comrade, either as a favour, or perhaps to repay a debt, he was 'taken down a peg'. A large measure was called a 'burra peg', while a small one was a 'chota peg'.

'Don't give a dam'   could not care less. A dam was a low denomination Indian coin, the local equivalent of a farthing. Thus not to give a dam was the Indian equivalent of the British expression, 'I really don't give a brass farthing'. *Brewers*

Dictionary of Phrase & Fable also makes a connection with the Latin word, *damnum*, meaning loss or injury.

'It was cold enough to freeze the balls off a brass monkey'   very chilly indeed. Royal Navy cannon balls were stacked in a frame, known as a 'brass monkey', which was similar to the triangle used to set up the red balls before a game of snooker, except that it was made of metal. In cold weather the metal contracts – and the balls fall off. *Brewer's Dictionary of Phrase & Fable* happily accepts this derivation while many consider it to be an 'urban myth'.

'Hoist with his own petard'   to be trapped in one's own snare. A petard was a bell- or box-shaped container, filled with explosive, designed to blow in the gate of a fortress, against which it was carefully positioned. The word is derived from the French, *péter*, which is used to describe an altogether more modest, albeit embarrassing, personal explosion. The job of a petardier was extremely dangerous: not only was he likely to be under heavy fire when placing his petard, and might perhaps be unable to withdraw swiftly enough – but the device also had an ominous tendency to explode prematurely, due to length of fuse or equipment malfunction, hence the expression.

'He's gone a bit barmy'   slightly mad. Oakwood Hospital at Barming Heath, near Maidstone (the main building of which was converted into luxury apartments in 2001–2) was founded in 1833 as Kent County Lunatic Asylum. Shell-shock, which is now known as Post-traumatic Stress Disorder (PTSD), was a major problem both during and after the First World War. Many sufferers received treatment at Oakwood Hospital and, although the word 'barmy' predated the outbreak of war, it gathered momentum during the war years. English cricket supporters who loyally follow their team on overseas tours are often described as members of 'the Barmy Army'.

'Cutting it a bit fine' almost too late. Cannonballs containing a secondary charge, such as shrapnel or common shell, rather than simple round shot, had a wooden fuse, ignited by the initial explosion when the round was fired. When the fuse was 'cut a bit fine', the consequences were similar to those of a poorly placed petard, as the round exploded prematurely, over the heads of the artilleryman's own men.

'Having a Mulley' finding time for a quick snooze. Having begun this section with one peer, I will close it with another. It is an unfortunate fact that some people are best remembered for a minor slip or indiscretion, rather than their many good works. As Secretary of State for Defence in 1977, the Labour politician, Frederick William (later Baron) Mulley, attended the Queen's Silver Jubilee Review of the Royal Air Force at RAF Finningley. Seated on the right of HM The Queen – and despite the constant noise of aircraft – Fred Mulley was caught on camera while having a quick, and rather public, kip. The Royal Air Force coined the expression, 'I'm just having a Mulley', for a sleep snatched under unpromising circumstances. *Private Eye* flippantly proposed that Mulley was guilty of treason, having slept with the Monarch.

BORROWED WORDS

The British Indian Empire lasted from 1757 to 1947, although there were British traders living in India before 1757 and quite a number 'stayed on', in Paul Scott's words, after

Independence on 15 August 1947. Although the Imperial Civil Service – popularly known as the Indian Civil Service – never employed many more than 1,000 people in its management structure, of whom two-thirds were British, there was a constant flow of soldiers, sailors and airmen and their families to and from the Indian subcontinent. Local words were absorbed into daily language and were then widely used in the British Isles, when 'old India hands' either retired, or were posted, home. The authority is *Hobson-Jobson: A Glossary of Colloquial Anglo-Indian Words and Phrases, and of Kindred Terms, Etymological, Historical, Geographical and Discursive*, by Henry (later Sir Henry) Yule and Arthur Coke Burnell, published by John Murray (London) in 1886. Some of the better-known examples include:

Baksheesh   from the Persian, *bakšiš*: beggars on the Indian subcontinent often plead: 'Baksheesh, baba!'

Bandanna   from the Hindustani, *bāndhnū*: a scarf tied round the head.

Batty   from the Hindustani, *bhātā*: wages; extra pay when on a campaign; or an additional allowance.

Bazaar   from the Persian, *bāzār*, meaning market. In Hindi, *lal kurti* means red jacket, as the soldiers were known to the locals. Regimental brothels, informally tolerated by the authorities, were known as *lal bazaars*.

Bhisty   from the Persian, *bihištī*, meaning a person of paradise: water-carrier; the eponymous hero of Rudyard Kipling's poem, 'Gunga Din', was a regimental bhisty.

Blighty   from the Hindustani, *bilāyatī*: foreign land. During the First World War, a 'Blighty one' was a wound that would not kill you, but was serious enough for you to be sent home for treatment. Three popular songs during the First World War were 'We Wish We Were In Blighty', 'There's A Ship That's Bound For Blighty' and 'Take Me Back To Dear Old Blighty, Put Me On The Train For London Town'.

Boche   the exception, since it is derived from the French, *caboche*: slang for cabbage head. During the First World War, German soldiers were known to their British counterparts as 'the Boche' and to the French Army as 'les sales Boches'.

Bundook   from the Hindustani, *bandūk*: a rifle or firearm.

Bungalow   from the Gujarati, *bangalo*, and the Hindustani, *banglā*, belonging to Bengal: a one-storeyed house, beloved of retired planters, and a feature of British ribbon development in the 1920s and 1930s.

Char   from the Hindustani, *char:* tea.

Charpoy   from the Hindustani, *chārpāī:* a bed.

Chitty or chit   from the Hindustani, *chitthī*: a letter or note.

Chokey   from the Hindustani, *caukī*, meaning shed: slang for military prison, otherwise known as 'the glasshouse'.

Chutney   from the Sanskrit, *caṭnī*, meaning to lick, and also the Hindustani, *chatni*, which refers specifically to sweet ground spices and condiments. Major Grey's Chutney, the recipe for which is thought to have been created by the eponymous Indian Army officer, is still manufactured in the United Kingdom and also on the subcontinent.

Coolie   from the Hindustani, *qulī*, but originally from the Portuguese, *cule*, used for locally hired labourers: unskilled manual labourer.

Cushy   from the Hindustani, *khush*: easy-going, soft, relaxed.

Dekko   from the Hindustani, *dekho*: look. *Dekho!* is the journal of The Burma Star Association.

Doolally   the Indian town of Deolali, in the Nashik district of Maharashtra, some 100 miles north-east of Mumbai (formerly Bombay), was a common staging post and collection centre for soldiers returning from India. Sometimes the travel warrants took such a frustratingly long time to come through that the soldiers were said to be suffering from 'doolally tap', meaning that they were either exhibiting slightly odd behaviour, or were perhaps completely out of their mind. Tap has its origins in the Sanskrit, *tapa*, meaning malarial fever.

Doolie   from the Hindustani, *ḍolī*, meaning a swing or cradle: a rudimentary ambulance.

Dungarees   from the Hindustani, *dungrī*, the name of a suburb of Bombay (now Mumbai), where coarse Indian calico given the same name was manufactured: a pair of overalls, with bib-and-braces, generally worn over normal clothing, in order to protect it.

Goolie   from the Hindustani, *golī*, meaning a pellet: a testicle.

Guru   from the Hindustani, *gurū*, meaning a Hindu spiritual teacher or the head of a sect.

Gymkhana   from the Hindustani, *jamat-khana*, meaning place of assembly: an equestrian event, typically involving a variety of disciplines.

Jeldi, juldee or jillo   from the Hindustani, *chalo*: to hurry up or look lively.

Jodhpurs   long riding breeches, tight from knee to ankle, named after the city of Jodhpur in the state of Rajasthan in northern India, where the Maharajah and members of his teams wore such trousers while playing polo. The word was first used in England in the 1890s, after the game had become popular.

Juggernaut   from the Hindustani, *Jagannath*, one of the names by which Krishna is known: an irresistible force or a large heavy truck or lorry.

Jungle   from the Hindustani, *jangal*, meaning overgrown ground.

Kedgeree   from the Hindustani, *khicrī*: a dish of rice and sesamum. In England, kedgeree is generally made with rice, fish, eggs and spices and is served hot.

Khaki   from the Hindustani, *khākī*: dust-coloured.

Loot   from the Hindustani, *lūt:* to plunder or sack.

Mufti   from the Arabic, *muftī*, meaning a Muslim scholar or official: plain clothes or 'civvies', rather than formal attire.

Mugger   from the Hindustani, *magar*, meaning the broad-nosed crocodile of India, which moves steathily.

Mulligatawny   from the Tamil, *miḷaku-taṇṇi*, meaning pepper water: a soup which can incorporate a variety of ingredients, including chicken, beef or lamb, seasoned with turmeric, which provides the traditional yellow colour.

Polo   from the Baltī, the language of the Indus Valley, *polo*, and the Tibetan, *pulu*: ball. The Calcutta Polo Club, the oldest in the world, was founded by two British officers, Captain Robert Stewart and Lieutenant (later Major General) Joseph Sherer, in 1862.

Pukka   from the Hindustani, *pakkā*, meaning cooked or substantial: genuine.

Punch   from the Hindustani, *pānch*, meaning five: a drink comprising five ingredients, traditionally alcohol, hot water or milk, sugar, flavoured with lemon and spices.

Pundit   from the Hindustani, *pandit*, meaning learned or skilled: an expert.

Tank   from the Gujarati *tankh*, meaning water cistern or reservoir. The word was introduced to Europe by the Portuguese in the sixteenth century and adopted in the First World War for the new fighting vehicle as a ruse so as not to arouse German suspicions. The British first used tanks at Flers-Courcelette during the Battle of the Somme on 15 September 1916. Three days later, *The Times* reported: '"Tanks" is what these new machines are generally called, and the name has the evident official advantage of being quite undescriptive.'

Thug   from the Hindustani, *thagī*, which refers to the system of murder and robbery practised by the so-called Thugs, who killed their victims by strangulation with a handkerchief, having first gained their confidence. The murders were highly ritualistic and were carried out in the name of the Hindu goddess, Kali, who was associated with violence and sexuality.

Tiffin   from the old English word, *tiffing*, meaning a small drink or sip: an Anglo-Indian word for elevenses or a light lunch.

Verandah   from the Hindustani, *varaṇḍā*, or the Portuguese, *varanda*.

Wallah   from the Hindustani, *-vālā*: which was adopted to refer to someone who provided a particular service, such as the punkah-wallah, who operated the fan, or the dhobi-wallah, who did the laundry. A competition-wallah was a successful candidate in the Indian Civil Service examinations, introduced after the Indian Mutiny of 1857–9, or the First War of Independence, depending on your point of view. A base-wallah was someone who stayed well behind the lines – in relative comfort and safety – during the First World War. Rather more poetically, a thief was known as a loose-wallah, while a padre was known as an amen-wallah.

On 31 July 1806, Major General Sir Arthur Wellesley (later the Duke of Wellington), who was then popularly known as 'the Sepoy General', following his distinguished generalship during a series of successful campaigns in India, wrote from Hastings to Lieutenant Colonel John Malcolm: 'I am a *nimmukwallah*, as we say in the East; that is, I have ate of the King's salt, and, therefore, I conceive it to be my duty to serve with unhesitating zeal and cheerfulness, when and wherever the King or his Government may think proper to employ me.' A number of threads are brought together by the nickname of the 3rd (King's Own) Light Dragoons, who so distinguished themselves at the Battle of Mudki on 18 December 1845 during the First Anglo-Sikh War that they became known as 'the Mudkiwallahs'.

❖

In Sir Tom Stoppard's 1995 play, *Indian Ink*, two characters compete – ever-so-slightly implausibly – to use as many
Hobson-Jobson words as possible in just a single sentence:

> Flora Crewe, an English poet: 'While having tiffin on the
> veranda of my bungalow, I spilled kedgeree on my dunga-
> rees and had to go to the gymkhana in my pyjamas looking
> like a coolie.'

> Nirad, an Indian artist: 'I was buying chutney in the bazaar
> when a thug who had escaped from the chokey ran amok
> and killed a box-wallah for his loot, creating a hullabaloo
> and landing himself in the mulligatawny.'

In fact, hullabaloo is not an Anglo-Indian word but makes
its first written appearance in Tobias Smollett's *Adventures of
Sir Launcelot Greaves* (1762): 'I would there was a blister on
this plaguy tongue of mine for making such a hollo-ballo.' It
may have its origins in the hunting field.

While serving in India during the 1930s, the 1st Battalion,
The Bedfordshire and Hertfordshire Regiment – known colloquially as 'The Beds an' Herts' – acquired a Hobson-Jobson
nickname, 'The Charps and Dils', where Charps is an abbreviation of *charpoy* and *dil* is the Hindustani for heart.

Ruth Prawer Jhabvala, who was actually of German
Jewish, and not Indian, extraction, as many people initially
thought, won the 1975 Booker Prize with her novel, *Heat
and Dust*. She was subsequently awarded two Oscars: for
her adapted screenplays for *A Room with a View* in 1986
and for *Howards End* in 1992. Before any of these triumphs,
though, she had collaborated with James Ivory and Ismail
Merchant on *Shakespeare Wallah* (1965) and *The Guru* (1969),

both of which use Hobson-Jobson titles. *Shakespeare Wallah* was loosely based on the adventures of Geoffrey Kendal and his travelling family theatre troupe of English actors, who performed Shakespeare's plays across India, in front of ever-dwindling audiences.

ARTICLES OF CLOTHING

The British Army, or officers serving therein, have given their names to a few items of clothing or accoutrements that, at one time at least, were extremely popular, even if only a handful now remain so. This is hardly a new subject. In their splendid *1066 And All That*, which was reprinted no fewer than seven times in November and December 1930, Walter Carruthers Sellar and Robert Julian Yeatman wrote: 'The troops in the Crimea suffered terribly from their Cardigans and Balaclava helmets and from a new kind of overcoat invented by Lord Raglan, the Commander-in-Chief.' As well as these three, there are other examples:

The Wellington boot   Dissatisfied with the prevailing fashion and finding his boots impractical and uncomfortable in 1817, after the defeat of Napoleon, the Duke of Wellington instructed his bootmaker, the fashionable George Hoby of St James's Street, London, to modify the eighteenth-century Hessian boot. The resulting boot was made from soft calfskin, had the trim removed and was specially cut to fit more closely around the leg. The heels were low cut and around an inch high, while the boot stopped at mid-calf, well below the knee. It was suitably hard-wearing for battle, yet comfortable for the evening. The tale is recounted in *A Short History of the*

Wellington Boot by Adam Edwards, published by Hodder & Stoughton (London) in 2006. It was clearly a profitable idea: after George Hoby was buried in the Nonconformist burial ground in Bunhill Fields on 17 February 1832, it was revealed that he had left a fortune of more than £13,300, the equivalent of more than £1,000,000 today.

The Raglan sleeve   On 18 June 1815 Lord Fitzroy Somerset, military secretary to the Duke of Wellington, was so seriously wounded in the right arm during the Battle of Waterloo that amputation, despite the attendant risks, was deemed to be the only solution. Following the loss of his arm, which did no harm at all to his military career, Lord Fitzroy Somerset asked his tailor to make him overcoats without shoulder seams, since they fitted him better. Their defining characteristic was to extend in one piece to the collar, leaving a diagonal seam from armpit to collarbone. Lord Fitzroy Somerset was raised to the Peerage as Baron Raglan on 20 October 1852 and sub-sequently commanded the British troops in the Crimea, until he died from dysentery – or perhaps from a broken heart, after the ignominious British failure to capture the Redan, the key to the Russian defences at Sebastopol – on 29 June 1855. According to Richard Rutt in *A History of Hand Knitting*, pub-lished in 1987 by Interweave Press, the above description of a Raglan sleeve first appeared in 1864, almost ten years after Lord Raglan's death.

The Cardigan   Brigadier General James Thomas Brudenell, 7th Earl of Cardigan, commanded the Light Cavalry Brigade during their ill-fated charge at the Battle of Balaclava on 25 October 1854, during the Crimean War. Military histori-ans are still arguing about the circumstances that preceded the charge, as well as about Cardigan's behaviour both during – and also after – the battle. Having spent most of the campaign on his steam yacht, *Dryad*, in Balaclava harbour, before being invalided home on 5 December 1854, before the worst of the winter weather had set in, it is somewhat surprising that he should have been commemorated by an article of clothing. Before his hasty departure, however, the sartorially adventurous and exceedingly vain Earl of Cardigan gave a new word to the English language, by wearing 'a knitted woollen over-waistcoat or jacket, with or without sleeves'. Unlike a pullover, a cardigan has buttons, or some other fastening, down the front. In memory of their controversial Colonel, the 11th Hussars always sounded Last Post at ten minutes to ten, the time of his death on 28 March 1868.

The Balaclava   The Crimean winter of 1854–5 was extremely harsh. On 12 January 1855, my great-grandfather, Lieutenant William Allan, 41st Regiment of Foot, wrote, in a letter home: 'Owing to the severe weather and hard work, the picquet and trench duties have, since the 3rd inst., been relieved every twelve hours instead of twenty-four. The men are having a rough time of it; some of them have had their toes frost-bitten.' On 19 February, however, he reported that 'the men are now well off, as heaps of various kinds of warm articles are showering in on them from all quarters'. It seems highly likely that some of these men had received woollen hats, which they could pull down to their shoulders, leaving only their eyes and mouth unprotected from the bitter cold and biting wind. Interestingly, there was no mention of the 'Balaclava helmet' – named after the British harbour and administrative base – during the war itself. According to Richard Rutt, the term was not introduced until 1881.

The Havelock   During the Indian Mutiny, Major General Sir Henry Havelock commanded the force that initially relieved the Siege of Lucknow on 25 September 1857, before they were once again besieged by the rebels. The Indian climate was dreadful for campaigning and, having spent most of his service there, Havelock was well aware of the risks, particularly of heat-stroke. A havelock is defined by *The Shorter Oxford English Dictionary* as 'a white cloth covering for the cap, with a flap hanging over the neck, worn by soldiers as a protection from the sun's heat'. Sadly, such precautions did not help Sir Henry, who died of dysentery – and exhaustion – at Dilkusha Park on 24 November 1857, just a week after the second raising of the siege. He was awarded a baronetcy, inherited by his eldest son, while both his wife and son were granted a pension of £1,000 a year by Parliament. His statue by William Behnes stands on one of the three occupied plinths in Trafalgar Square.

The haversack   The English word, haversack, is derived from the German, *Habersack*, or oat bag, in which oats for the horses were carried. Eighteenth-century recruiting sergeants operating in the West Riding of Yorkshire used to brandish havercakes on the end of their swords, in order to reassure anxious recruits that they would not be going hungry, a practice which led to the 33rd Regiment of Foot, later The Duke of Wellington's Regiment, being given the nickname, 'The Havercake Lads'. The white linen shoulder-bag in which soldiers carried their rations became known as a haversack, the ancestor of the ubiquitous backpack, the unsympathetic wearing of which can often make it impossible to turn round on a crowded London Underground train.

SURPRISING SHIPS

When judged by modern standards, the Royal Navy has chosen some rather unusual names for its ships over the centuries:

HMS *Beaver*   a Royalist ketch (1656–8); a former 18-gun French sloop (1757–61); a 14-gun sloop (1761–83); a 14-gun sloop (1795–1808); a 10-gun Cherokee-class sloop (1809–29); a wooden paddle packet (1837–45); an Albacore-class wooden screw gunboat (1855–64); a 125-ton tender (1905–11); an Acheron-class destroyer (1911–21); a Type 22 frigate (1982–2001)

HMS *Cockchafer*   a former 5-gun American schooner tender (1812–15); an Albacore-class wooden screw gunboat

(1855–72); a Banterer-class composite screw gunboat (1881–1905); an Insect-class gunboat (1915–49)

HMS *Gay Bruiser* (P1044)   a Gay-class fast patrol boat (1952–62)

HMS *Gay Dragoon* (P1050)   a Gay-class fast patrol boat (1953–62)

HMS *Gay Viking* (MGB-506)   a motor gunboat (1943–5)

HMS *Spanker* a 24-gun floating battery (1794–1810); an Albacore-class wooden screw gunboat (1856–74); a Sharpshooter-class torpedo gunboat (1889–1920); an Algerine-class minesweeper (1943–7)

HMS *Thrasher* a T-class submarine (1940–7)

Not to be outdone, the US Navy put into service:

USS *Chopper* (SS-342)   a Balao-class submarine (1945–69)

USS *Flasher* (SS-249)   a Gato-class submarine (1943–59)

USS *Saucy* a Flower-class corvette (1942–5); formerly HMS *Arabis* and subsequently HMS *Snapdragon*

It transpires that this is a game that the Merchant Navy can play just as well, albeit from rather different angles, with:

SS *Iron Knob* a 3,349 gross registered tonnage (GRT) Australian cargo ship, owned by BHP Shipping (1923–55)

SS *Lesbian* a 2,352 GRT British cargo ship, owned by Ellerman Lines (1923–41)

Advice

'Advice is always dangerous, but good advice is fatal'
– Oscar Wilde

*'To profit from good advice requires more wisdom
than to give it'* – John Churton Collins

FROM FATHER TO SON

In 1804 Rear-Admiral Sir Edward Pellew, later 1st Viscount Exmouth, wrote to his eldest son, Commander Pownoll Bastard Pellew, who had recently assumed command of his first ship, the 18-gun sloop, *Fly*:[1]

From your Affectionate Father to his Dutiful Son,

Avoid as certain destruction both of Soul and Body all excess of whatever Nature they may be. In the Climate you are going to [the West Indies] you must use great Caution to avoid all the night dews – and when you are exposed by night never permit your breast to be uncovered or your neck exposed without something tied round it. Never stop on Deck unless covered by something to keep off the dew. It is equally necessary to avoid the Sun in the Middle of the Day from which much danger is to be expected. It may at a moment produce Giddyness of head, sickness and fever. Take great care never to over-heat your blood by drinking or exercise. Never go out shooting on any account or riding in the Sun and be very particular never to check perspiration or sit in a draft of Wind so as to produce it – although it is so pleasant to the feeling it is almost certain Death.

At night always sleep in Calico. Be you ever so hot, it is a great security against the diseases of that Country. On your first arrival be extremely careful not to indulge in eating too much fruit – and do not go into the water when the Sun is high. Take great care to keep your body regular and never pass a day without Evacuation. The moment you feel your Body bound take directly a pill or two of those you carry of the size of a large pea.

---

[1] Stephen Taylor, *Commander: The Life and Exploits of Britain's Greatest Frigate Captain*, London: Faber and Faber Ltd, 2012, pp. 308–10.

And should you ever feel unwell instantly take a strong Emetic or a good dose of Physic. If you are seized with a flux take directly a large dose of Rhubarb and apply directly to your Surgeon. Always wear a piece of White paper inside your hat.

If you should take prizes I need scarcely recommend you to treat your Prisoners with kindness, but be very careful to keep safe and proper Guards over them. An Officer who suffers his Prisoners to retake his Ship can never recover the Stain on his Character.

Be extremely Cautious and Correct in your Conduct. The first impression of your Character will form from it and the companions of your choice. Always endeavour to keep in with the Captains and Admiral as much as possible, behaving with quiet Modesty. You will always learn something in their Company and they will soon respect and esteem you.

Never become one of the Tavern parties on shore. They always end in drunkenness and Dissipation.

In your Command be as kind as you can without suffering imposition on your good Nature. Be steady and vigilant. Never neglect any opportunity to write to your Mother who deserves your utmost love and attention for her unceasing goodness to you and all your family. I hope you will believe I shall be equally glad to hear of you. I am sure you will never dishonour yourself or your family or the Service of your King.

In your Expenses be as frugal as you can. You know the situation of your Father and how many calls he has for Money, and should you have any of your own to send to England I recommend your sending it to Wedderburn. Be attentive to your person and dress. Nothing recommends a young Man more to notice. If you meet Capt O'Brien tell him I ordered you to ask his protection. Admiral Dacres will be as a Father to you. Never fail to consult him and ask his advice on any occasion of difficulty. Take great care to examine all papers you put your name to and be satisfied of the truth of them and avoid any accident on this point. Never sign a paper when brought to you in a hurry if it is one of account but desire it to be left to your perusal. At least once a month look over your Ship's Books and the different officers' expenses – and do not pass by any extraordinary expense without strictly investigating the circumstance, as it is your Duty to be as honest and careful for the King as for yourself.

Never fail to keep the Ship's reckoning yourself and observe by Day and Night. It is a great Duty for you have in charge the Lives of hundreds. I hope you will never from idleness excuse yourself from this sacred Duty and never lay down to rest without sending for your Master and together with him mark the Ship's place in the Chart. Do not let any false Modesty or Shame prevent you from this or asking his aid in working your Lunars. It is madness to do so in the extreme and must ultimately end in the ruin of any Young Officer who practises it.

Whether Pownoll heeded his father's advice is debatable since, just a year later, the *Fly* was lost on a reef, although all the members of the crew were saved. Commander Pellew was found 'not guilty' of negligence by the resulting, mandatory court martial. Failing to achieve great success in the Royal Navy, however, he resigned his commission and served as Member of Parliament for Launceston in Cornwall from 1812 to 1830. Succeeding his father as 2nd Viscount Exmouth on 23 January 1833, Pownoll survived him by less than a year, dying on 3 December. How he acquired his second name – while still inheriting the title – remains a slight mystery!

Sir George Sitwell, author of *An Essay on the Making of Gardens*, published in 1909 by John Murray, wrote to his eldest

son, who was then serving with The Grenadier Guards, on
14 December 1914:[2]

My dear Osbert,

As I fear a line sent to Chelsea Barracks may not reach you
before you leave tomorrow, I write to you care of your regiment, B.E.F. [British Expeditionary Force] so that you may find a
letter waiting for you when you arrive in the trenches. But I had
wanted if possible to give you a word of advice before you left.
Though you will not, of course, have to encounter anywhere
abroad the same weight of gunfire that your mother and I had
to face here [when the High Seas Fleet bombarded Scarborough]
– it has been my contention for many years that there were
no guns in the world to compare for weight and range with
the great German naval guns, and that our own do not come
anywhere near them – yet my experience may be useful to you.
Directly you hear the first shell, retire, as I did, to the undercroft,
and remain there quietly until all firing has ceased. Even then, a
bombardment, especially as one grows older, is a strain upon the
nervous system – but the best remedy for that, as always, is to
keep warm and have plenty of plain, nourishing food at frequent
but regular intervals. And, of course, plenty of rest. I find a nap
in the afternoon most helpful, if not unduly prolonged, and I
advise you to try it wherever possible.

In the noisy, dangerous and distracting environment of trench
warfare, Osbert Sitwell somehow found the inspiration to write
his first poetry. His appropriately entitled poem, 'Babel', was
printed in *The Times* on 11 May 1916.

---

[2] John Julius Norwich, *A Christmas Cracker: Being a Commonplace
Selection*, published privately, 2012.

TO YOUNG OFFICERS

The Armed Services offer a particularly rich seam to mine for those in pursuit of advice and satire, largely as a consequence of comradeship, continuity and ever-threatening confusion. *Advice to the Officers of the British Army with the Addition of Some Hints to the Drummer and Soldier*, which was written anonymously but attributed to Francis Grose, while reflecting the recent loss of the American colonies, and first published in 1782, was reprinted by Jonathan Cape (London) in 1946:

> Those who are unacquainted with the service may perhaps imagine, that this chapter is addressed to the subalterns only – but a little knowledge of the present state of the British forces will soon convince them, that it comprehends not only the greatest part of the captains, but also many of the field officers, of the army.
>
> The first article we shall consider is your dress; a taste in which is the most distinguishing mark of a military genius, and the principal characteristic of a good officer.
>
> Ever since the days of Antient Pistol, we find, that a large broad-brimmed beaver has been peculiar to heroes. A hat of this kind worn over your right eye, with two large dangling tassels, and a proportionate cockade and feather, will give you an air of courage and martial gallantry.
>
> The fashion of your clothes must depend on that ordered in the corps; that is to say, must be in direct opposition to it: for it would show a deplorable poverty of genius if you had not some ideas of your own in dress.
>
> Your cross-belt should be broad, with a huge blade pendent to it – to which you may add a dirk and a bayonet, in order to give you the more tremendous appearance.
>
> Thus equipped you sally forth, with your colours, or chitterlin,

advanced and flying; and I think it will be best in walking through the streets, particularly if they are narrow, to carry your sword in your right hand. For besides its having a handsome and military appearance, the pommel of the sword will serve to open you a free passage, by shoving it in the guts of every one who does not give way. He must be a bold man who will venture to oppose you; as by your dress he cannot in reason expect the least quarter. We are told that the Janissaries never wear their swords but upon duty; a practice more becoming Turks than Christians.

When you visit your friends either in town or country, or make an excursion to any other place where your regiment is not known, immediately mount two epaulets, and pass yourself for a grenadier officer.

Never wear your uniform in quarters, when you can avoid it. A green or a brown coat shows you have other clothes beside your regimentals, and likewise that you have courage to disobey a standing order. If you have not an entire suit, at least mount a pair of black breeches, a round hat, or something unregimental and unmilitary.

If you belong to a mess, eat with it as seldom as possible, to let folks see that you want neither money nor credit. And when you do, in order to show that you are used to good living, find fault with every dish that is set on the table, damn the wine, and throw the plates at the mess-man's head.

If the dinner is not served up immediately on your sitting down, draw circles with your fork on the table; cut the table-cloth; and, if you have pewter plates, spin them on the point of your fork, or do some other mischief, to punish the fellow for making you wait.

On coming into the regiment, perhaps the major or adjutant will advise you to learn the manual, the salute, or other parts of the exercise; to which you may answer, that you do not want to be drill-sergeant or corporal – or that you purchased your commission and did not come into the army to be made a machine of.

It will also be perfectly needless for you to consult any treatises of military discipline, or the regulations for the army. Dry books of tactics are beneath the notice of a man of genius, and it is a known fact, that every British officer is inspired with a perfect knowledge of his duty, the moment he gets his commission; and if he were not, it would be sufficiently acquired in *conversaziones* at the main-guard or the grand sutler's. Thus a general officer, who had never before seen a day's service beyond the limits of Blackheath or Wimbledon common, being ordered abroad, lands in America or Germany a *factus imperator*, though by very different means from those of Lucullus. If you have a turn for reading, or find it necessary to kill in that manner the tedious hours in camp or garrison, let it be such books as warm the imagination and inspire to military achievements, as, *The Woman of Pleasure*, *Crazy Tales*, *Rochester's Poems*; if you aim at solid instruction and useful knowledge, you must study *Lord Chesterfield's Letters*, or *Truster's Politeness*; if you have a turn for natural philosophy, you may peruse *Aristotle's Master-piece*; and the *Trials of Adultery* will afford you a fund of historical and legal information.

If there should be a soberly-disposed person, or, in other words, a fellow of no spirit, in the corps, you must not only *bore* him constantly at the mess, but should make use of a kind of practical wit to torment him. Thus you may force open his doors, break his windows, damage his furniture, and put wh---s in his bed; or in camp throw squibs and crackers into his tent at night, or loosen his tent-cords in windy weather. Young gentlemen will never be at a loss for contrivances of this nature.

Be sure also to stigmatise every officer, who is attentive to his duty, with the appellation of *Martinet*; and say he has been bitten by a mad adjutant. This will discourage others from knowing more than yourself, and thereby keep you upon an equality with them. When ordered for duty, always grumble and question the roster. This will procure you the character of one that will not be imposed on. At a field day, be sure not to fall in before the regiment is told off and proved; and then come upon the parade, buttoning your gaiters, or putting on some part of your dress. Observe the same when for guard – making 20 or 30 men wait, shows you are somebody.

Whenever you mount guard, invite all your friends to the guardroom; and not only get drunk yourself, but make your company drunk also; and then sing and make as much noise as possible. This will show the world the difference between an officer and a private man; since the latter would be slayed alive for the least irregularity upon duty.

Though it may, on some occasions, be proper and becoming a military man, to be watchful and to sit up all night, as in drinking, gaming, at a masquerade, etc., yet it would be an intolerable bore on guard; and, if near an enemy, and liable to be attacked, would argue a degree of apprehension that a good soldier should be ashamed of.

When a guard mounts with colours, they will make a handsome covering for the card-table at night, and will prevent it from becoming stained or soiled.

When you mount the quarterguard in camp, as soon as the men have grounded their arms, put off your sash and gorget, and immediately go to your tent, or to the grand sutler's in the rear. The sergeant can take charge of the men in your absence; and should any General officers happen to come by, you will have an opportunity to shew your activity, in running across the parade in order to turn out the guard.

Never read the daily orders. It is beneath an officer of spirit to bestow any attention upon such nonsense; and the information you can get from them will not repay you for the trouble you are at in deciphering them and reducing them into English. It will be sufficient to ask the sergeant if you are for any duty.

Be a constant attendant at the General officer's levees. If you get nothing else by it, you may at least learn how to scrape and bow, to simper and to display a handsome set of teeth, by watching closely the conduct of the aid-de-camp.

At exercise you must be continually thrusting out your spontoon, ordering the men to dress, and making as much noise as possible; in order to show your attention to your duty.

When at a field day or review, you have taken post in the rear for the manual exercise to be performed, you have a fine opportunity of diverting yourselves and the spectators. You stand very convenient for playing at leap-frog, or may pelt one

another with stones; or, if there should be snow on the ground, with snowballs. This will be a very harmless relaxation, as you have nothing else to do, and besides the diversion it will afford among yourselves, will contribute vastly to amuse the soldiers and to prevent them from puzzling their brains too much with the business they are about.

If you are in the right wing during the firings, you must always keep a pace or two in front, till you order the men to fire, when it will be expedient for you to step into the rear, to prevent your face from being scorched with the powder; or you may order two or three file on the right of your platoon to do only the motions of firing, which, if it diminishes the fire of the battalion, will at least save His Majesty's ammunition.

Evening roll-calling, which drags one from the bottle, is a most unmilitary custom: for drinking is as essential a part of an officer's duty as fighting. Thus Alexander prided himself more on being able to take off half a dozen bottles at a sitting, than on all his victories over the army of Darius. If the Colonel then should insist on the attendance of the officers they should not fail to get a little mellow first, to show the world that they are no milk-sops; but if any of the soldiers should presume to imitate their example, they must be confined and brought to a courtmartial; for what is commendable in an officer may be in the highest degree reprehensible in a private man; and, as the dramatic poet observes:

That in the captain's but a hasty word,
Which in the soldier is rank blasphemy.

When you are ordered to visit the barracks, I would recommend it to you to confine your inspection to the outside walls: for what can be more unreasonable than to expect, that you should enter the soldier's dirty rooms, and contaminate yourself with tasting their messes? As you are not used to eat salt pork or ammunition bread, it is impossible for you to judge whether they are good or not. Act in the same manner, when ordered to visit the hospital. It is none of your business to nurse and attend the sick. Besides, who knows but you might catch some infectious distemper? And it would be better that fifty soldiers should perish through neglect or bad treatment than the King should lose a good officer.

Always use the most opprobrious epithets in reprimanding the soldiers, particularly men of good character: for these men it will not in the least hurt, as they will be conscious that they do not deserve them.

When on leave of absence, never come back to your time; as that might cause people to think, that you had nowhere to stay, or that your friends were tired of you.

Make trenches round your marquis in camp, to carry off the water, and to prevent the stray-horses from coming near enough to tread upon your tent-cords. The larger and deeper they are, the better; that such as stumble into them in the night may break their legs, which will be a useful warning to the other horses.

If ever you have been abroad, though but to deliver drafts at Emden or Williamstadt, give yourself the airs of an experienced veteran; and in particular find fault with all parades, field days, and reviews, as of no consequence on real service. In regard to all these, say you hate to be *playing at soldiers*.

TO THE PRIVATE SOLDIER

Francis Grose continued:

As a private soldier, you should consider all your officers as your natural enemies, with whom you are in a perpetual state of warfare: you should reflect that they are constantly endeavouring to withhold from you all your just dues, and to impose on you every unnecessary hardship; and this for the mere satisfaction of doing you an injury. In your turn, therefore, make it a point to deceive and defraud them, every possible opportunity; and more particularly the officers of the company to which you belong.

First then, take every method of getting into your captain's debt; and, when you are pretty handsomely on his books, turn out a volunteer for foreign service, or else desert; and after waiting for a proclamation, or an act of grace, surrender yourself to some other corps.

On duty, as soon as the corporal has posted you sentry, and left you (if he has given himself the trouble of coming out with the relief), endeavour to accommodate yourself as conveniently as you can, the health of every good soldier being of the utmost consequence to the service. For this purpose, if you have a sentry-box, get some stones, and make yourself a seat; or bore two large holes in the opposite sides, through which you may pass your stick, or for want of it, your firelock. Thus seated, in order that you may not fall asleep, which would be rather improper and dangerous for a sentry, sing or whistle some merry tune, as loud as possible: this will both keep you awake, and convince people that you really are so.

In camp, where you cannot have the benefit of a box, as soon as you are posted, carefully ground your arms in some dry place, a good soldier being always careful of his arms; and, wrapping yourself up in your watch-coat, sit or lie down in the lee of some officer's marquis; and, to pass the tedious hours away, whistle or sing, as before directed; and if ever you smoke, there cannot be a better time to take a pipe.

If you are sentinel at the tent of one of the field-officers, you need not challenge in the fore part of the evening, for fear of disturbing his honour, who perhaps may be reading, writing, or entertaining company. But as soon as he is gone to bed, roar out every ten minutes at least, *Who comes there?* though nobody is passing. This will give him a favourable idea of your alertness; and though his slumbers may be broken, yet will they be the more pleasing, when he finds that he reposes in perfect security. When the hour of relief approaches, keep constantly crying out, *Relief! relief!* it will prevent the guard from forgetting you, and prove that you are not asleep.

Perhaps it may be unnecessary to inform you that in relieving you may go without your arms and take the firelock from the man you relieve. By this contrivance none of the firelocks, but those of the sentries, will be wet, or out of order.

On a march, should you be one of the baggage guard, put your arms, knapsack, and haversack on the waggon; and if they are lost, or your firelock broken, make out some story to your captain, who at all events must replace and repair them.

Should you, by accident, have pawned or sold your necessaries, feign sickness on the day they are reviewed, and borrow those of any soldier, whose company is not inspected. You may, in your turn, oblige him in the like manner; and, if this cannot be done, contrive to get confined for some trivial neglect, till the review is over.

If your comrade deserts, you may safely sell your whole kit, and charge him with having stolen it: should he be caught, and deny it, nobody will believe him.

If the duty runs hard, you may easily sham sick, by swallowing a quid of tobacco. Knock your elbow against the wall, or your tent-pole, and it will accelerate the circulation to the quickness of a fever. Quick lime and soap will give you a pair of sore legs, that would deceive the surgeon-general himself: and the rheumatism is an admirable pretence, not easily discovered. If you should be sent to a hospital in London, contrive to draw money from the agent; it is your officer's business to look to the payment.

When you are really taken ill, flap your hat, let your hair hang loose upon your shoulders, wear a dirty handkerchief about your neck, unhook your skirts, and ungaiter your stockings. These are all privileges of sickness.

If your mess have changed their marketing for gin, or any other good liquor, and have nothing to put into the pot, carefully wrap up a puppy or a brickbat in a cloth, and call it a sheep's head, or a pudding. This you may very safely do, as it is a hundred to one that your officer will not be at the pains to examine it.

At a field-day, stop up the touchhole of your piece with cobbler's wax, or some other substance. This will prevent your firing, and save you the trouble of cleaning your arms: besides, unless the quarter-master-sergeant and his pioneers are uncommonly careful, you may secrete some cartridges to sell to the boys of the town to make squibs.

In the firings always be sure to fill your pan as full of powder as possible; it will cause much fun in the ranks, by burning your right-hand man: and on the right wing it will also burn the officers; who, perhaps, to save their pretty faces, may order the right-hand file of each platoon not to fire, and thus save them the trouble of dismounting their firelocks and washing the barrel after the exercise is over.

In coming down as front rank, be sure to do it briskly, and let the toe of the butt first touch the ground. By this you may possibly break the stock; which will save the trouble of further exercise that day: and your captain will be obliged to make good the damage.

When you want to screw in a fresh flint, do it with your bayonet: if this notches it, it will be useful as a saw, and you will, besides, show your ingenuity in making it serve for purposes for which it never was intended: though, indeed, this weapon may be said to be the most handy of any a soldier carries. It is an excellent instrument for digging potatoes, onions, or turnips. Stuck in the ground, it makes a good candlestick; and it will on occasion serve either to kill a mudlark, or to keep an impertinent boot at a proper distance, whilst your comrades are gathering his apples.

Should you get to be an officer's servant, you may immediately commence fine gentleman. If he is about your own size, you may wear his shirts and stockings; and should you tear them in putting them on, it is his fault for having them made so small.

When he is on guard, you may invite company to his marquis, and it is hard if you cannot get a key that will open his canteens.

If on the march he gives you a canteen with a lock to carry, this is truly muzzling the ox; which is forbidden in scripture. You may therefore punish him by breaking the bottle and drinking his liquor: there will be no difficulty to bring witnesses to prove it was done by a fall.

When you wait on him at the mess, you may easily contrive to pocket half a fowl, a duck, a tongue, or some such convenient morsel; and you and your brethren must be very awkward and improvident if you can't filch some beer, or a bottle of wine, to drink with it. Some sutlers are kind enough to poor servants to score a pot or two of ale for their benefit.

If you are batman to an officer, your perquisites are certain. Sell half the forage to the sutlers who keep horses or asses: if they don't pay you in money, they will in gin. As a Christian is more worthy than a beast, it is better your master's horses should want than you.

When in quarters, should your landlord be uncivil, there are various methods by which you may bring him to reason. If he refuses to subsist you at the rated allowance, you may soon force him to it by roasting a cat, a dog, or an old boot, at the landlord's fire: for it is no business of his what you dress for your own dinner.

You may be sure that, go into what quarters you will, the landlord will heartily wish you out of them. You should therefore

make it a point to give him good cause for it; as it is hard a man
should be hated and despised without reason.

TO A SOLDIER FROM
THE REVEREND JOHN WESLEY

The Methodist movement held a natural appeal for those
who felt excluded from the established church, such as non-
commissioned soldiers and sailors. The founder of Methodism,
the Reverend John Wesley, preached his first open-air, 'fire
and brimstone' sermon in Bristol in 1739. At the time of the
Second Jacobite Rebellion, which culminated in the Battle of
Culloden on 16 April 1746, Wesley wrote *A Word in Season, or
Advice to a Soldier*, in which he included the following thought-
provoking passage:

Are you to die? Must you leave this world, and carry nothing
of it away with you? Naked as you came out of your mother's
womb, naked shall you return. Are you never to come back into
this world? Have you no more place under the sun? When you
leave these houses and fields, this flesh and blood, do you part
with them for ever? Are you sure of this? Must all men die? Can
none at all escape death? Do rich men likewise die, and leave
their riches for others? Do princes also fall and die like one of
their people? Can you then escape it? ...

Will you reply to all this: 'But I am a soldier, and have therefore nothing to do with these things.' Hold! Have soldiers
nothing to do with death? How so? Do soldiers never die? Can
you fright death away? No, my friend; he will not regard all your
big words and looks, nor all the weapons of your warfare. You
can neither conquer nor escape him. Your profession may excuse
you from many other things; but there is no excusing yourself

from death. Are you less sure of this than other men are? No; there is one lot for all. Are you farther from it than they? Nay, rather nearer; you live in the very jaws of death. Why, then, a soldier (if there be any difference) has more to do with death than other men. It is not far from every one of us; but to him it is just at the door.

Or do you fancy a soldier has nothing to do with judgment? Will you say, then, (as poor Captain Uratz did, when he was asked a few minutes before his death, if he had made his peace with God,) 'I hope God will deal with me like a gentleman?' But God said unto him, 'Thou fool! I will deal with thee as with all mankind. There is no respect of persons with me. I reward every man according to his works.' Thou also shalt receive of the righteous Judge according to the things which thou hast done in the body. Death levels all; it mingles in one dust the gentleman, soldier, clown, and beggar; it makes all these distinctions void. When life ends, so do they. Holy or unholy, is the one question then. Lo! the books are opened, that all the dead may be judged according to the things that are written therein. O may thy name be found written in the book of life!

For have soldiers nothing to do with hell? Why, then, is it so often in thy mouth? Dost thou think God does not hear the prayer? And how often hast thou prayed to him to damn thy soul? Is his ear waxed heavy, that it cannot hear? I fear thou wilt find it otherwise. Was he not a soldier, too, (and a terrible one,) to whom God said of old, 'Hell from beneath is moved for thee, to meet thee at thy coming?' And what marvel? For sin is the high road to hell. And have soldiers nothing to do with sin? Alas! how many of you wallow therein, yea, and glory in your shame! How do you labour to work out your own damnation! O, poor work for poor wages! The wages of sin is death; the wages of cursing, of swearing, of taking the name of God in vain, of Sabbath breaking, drunkenness, revenge, of fornication, adultery, and all uncleanness. Now, are thou clear of these? Does not thine own heart smite thee? Art thou not condemned already? What voice is that which sounds in thine ears? Is it not the voice of God? 'Shall I not visit for these things, saith the Lord. Shall not my soul be avenged on such a sinner as this?' It is a fearful thing to fall into the hands of the living God! Be very sure that thou art stronger than he, before thou fliest in his face! Do not defy God, unless thou canst overcome him. But canst thou indeed? Oh no; do not try. Do not dare him to do his worst. Why should he destroy both thy body and soul in hell? Why shouldest thou be punished with everlasting destruction from the presence of the Lord, and from the glory of his power?

But if there were no other hell, thou hast hell enough within thee. An awakened conscience is hell. Price, envy, wrath, hatred, malice, revenge; what are these but hell upon earth? And how often are thou tormented in these flames! – flames of lust, envy, or proud wrath! Are not these to thy soul, when blown up to the height, as if it were a lake of fire, burning with brimstone? Flee away, before the great gulf is fixed; escape, escape for thy life! If thou hast not strength, cry to God, and thou shalt receive power from on high; and He whose name is rightly called Jesus shall save thee from thy sins.

And why should he not? Has a soldier nothing to do with heaven? God forbid that you should think so! Heaven was designed for you also. God so loved your soul, that he gave his only-begotten Son, that you, believing in him, might not perish, but have everlasting life. Receive, then, the kingdom prepared for you from the foundation of the world! This, this is the time to make it sure; this short, uncertain day of life. Have you then an hour to spare? No; not a moment. Arise, and call upon thy God. Call upon the Lamb, who taketh away the sins of the world, to take away thy sins. Surely he hath borne thy griefs and carried thy sorrows! He was wounded for thy transgressions, and bruised for thy iniquities. He hath paid the ransom for thy soul. Believe in him, and thou shalt be saved. Art thou a sinner?

He came not to call the righteous, but sinners, to repentance. Art thou a lost, undone sinner? He came to seek and to save that which was lost. May He that gave himself for thee, give thee ears to hear, and a heart to understand, his love! So shalt thou also say, 'The life I now live, I live by faith in the Son of God.' So shall the love of God be shed abroad in thy heart, and thou shalt rejoice with joy unspeakable. Thou shalt have the mind that was in Christ, and shalt so walk as he also walked; till, having fought the good fight, and finished thy course, thou receive the crown that fadeth not away!

HINTS, SUBALTERNS, FOR USE OF

Although the profession of arms is inherently serious, the frequently ludicrous situations in which the participants find themselves keep the topic ever fresh – and adapted to the changing nature of things. In this context, *Hints, Subalterns, for Use of* is not so easy to tie down precisely, for obvious reasons. The Army reference is BF/OOL and the 1st edition was dated 1 April 1899, which rather gives the game away. I have a copy of the 9th edition, apparently revised in December 1943. All that can be said with confidence is that it was printed in England by C. H. Gee & Co. Ltd, 5/9 Great Central Street, Leicester.

The pamphlet describes itself as 'A collection of Maxims gathered in a short and undistinguished career with the old volunteers, regulars and new armies during peace and war. They do not claim to be original or new but, like port, are none the worse for that. If you read to the end you will certainly find the joke that made you kick the bottom out of your cradle. It is nice meeting old friends.' What follows is an edited version:

MAXIMS FOR A SUBALTERN

On first joining your regiment ASK for leave. You won't get it. Don't let this deter you. Go on asking and after a time it will become your prospective right.

Don't think for yourself. Ask the Adjutant. He is paid to think for you.

You are told to cultivate self-reliance and initiative. Don't believe a word of it. The first is almost insubordination and the second amounts to mutiny.

The Senior Officer is always right till one senior to him comes along and disagrees with him. The Senior Officer is still right.

Never disagree with a senior officer however wrong he may be. If he disagrees with you, above all things never prove yourself right. The first is conduct subservient to good order and military discipline, but the latter disgraceful conduct unbecoming an officer and a gentleman.

Never be cheery at breakfast. If you are too young to have acquired a liver, remember you soon will. Many a man has got a cracked jaw for a better joke than you will ever crack.

Only two subjects are allowed to be discussed at Mess in a 'good' regiment. Women (not ladies) and horses. Anything else is shop or tends towards culture, in which a junior might tend to show his superiority. This would be bad for discipline. The two subjects allowed are safe, for of the former they know nothing and of the latter very little more. Perhaps motor cars and 'bikes' have dethroned the horse, but that does not alter the truth of the above.

Originality in thought or dress or anything else is taboo and no more tolerated off parade and out of uniform than it would be on or in it. This is why you wear a uniform, not to distinguish you from the enemy, but to make you look and think as much alike as possible.

The value of your opinion on any subject, military or otherwise, depends, not on your knowledge of the subject, but on the number of years' service you have had.

If you choose to be thoroughly efficient and keen on your job, no one will mind or interfere with you as long as you conceal the fact decently.

If you come from the University, your brother officers will strike you as narrow and stupid. Don't worry. In ten years you will be just as narrow and probably more stupid.

It is often better to incur a mild reprimand than perform an arduous duty; but not too often.

When ordered to 'show interest' in the men's pastimes, show it. You never know when it mayn't be a matter of life and death whether they show interest in you or not. Your afternoon is spoilt anyhow.

Never do to-day what can be done to-morrow. Some fool may do it for you in the meantime.

Never do anything you can get anyone else to do for you.

Always be kind to the last joined subaltern. He will never forget it and be more willing to do your duty before you are senior enough to make him.

Show great dash on hot field days. It will get you a reputation for enterprise and many a quiet hour's rest when put out of action.

Always pity the General at the Annual Inspection. He is much more bored at it than you are. You have only one a year. He is always at it. He must find some fault, so make it easy for him.

A cigarette card on the parade ground, a rifle the wrong way in the rack, a loaf of bread in the wrong place. Any of these under his nose will be enough for him and prevent him finding out your real deficiencies and inefficiencies.

A lie is a very present help in trouble, so tell the truth often so that your lie may be believed.

Always have a ready answer. You can never be quite sure the questioner knows the right one.

You can lose anything you like at cards except your temper. This privilege is reserved for field officers only; below that rank it shows lack of breeding.

Never look a horse in the mouth or a general in the eye. Both will bite you. One because he resents the familiarity, the other because he knows you are about to lie.

If you are scored off, laugh louder than anyone. It takes the sting out of it, and thus disarming your opponent makes it easy for you to get your own back, if you think it is worth while to. Generally it isn't.

An ounce of sportsmanship is worth a pound of learning. The soldier understands one and suspects the other.

KIT INSPECTION

Anything black and shiny in a blacking tin IS 'blacking'.

One pair of socks is three pairs. One on; one at wash; one present. To ask a man to show the other one is ungentlemanly. A rolled up shirt which is stitched up should never be examined. The man has taken pains to prevent it and 'show a neat kit'. His trouble should be respected. A comment on any of the above will not be resented and will be understood to mean: 'this must not occur again.'

Respect the sanctity of the barrack room glory hole until it smells. There will always be one, and the less it is hidden the less likely it is to become a nuisance.

Never overlook anything without letting the individual know you have shut the other eye. Thus you will get a reputation for wisdom, which will save you a lot of trouble.

HANDING OVER

Do unto others as they would do unto you, but do it first.

Short drinks save long correspondence.

A water-bottle has become a water-cart before now by getting on the wrong Army Form.

No barracks have ever been handed over dirty or taken over clean.

'Thou shalt not steal' from any unit in your own brigade. They live too close to make it worth while.

The first duty of an officer is to see to his men's food and comfort, his second duty to see to his own. Any damn fool can be uncomfortable.

There are some men who believe that you can't be an efficient soldier without being thoroughly uncomfortable yourself and making everyone around you the same. These queer specimens are sometimes found amongst the Guards, but more often are Territorials, never in the cavalry. This disease is incurable and on active service always ends fatally.

Never miss an opportunity to take yourself easy. You never know when you will get the next. (Duke of Wellington's advice to his godson on joining his regiment.)

Unless you contemplate suicide or enjoy accidents never be sarcastic with your men. They don't understand it and will hate you for it. Sarcasm is the weapon of the weak against the strong.

If you must swear, swear into the blue, not at any particular individual. He may be a sea lawyer [argumentative person].

Swearing will never make you unpopular and, if you invent any new words, will earn you admiration in a hard swearing regiment. But this will be difficult. Remember the soldiers swore terribly in Flanders. That was not in 1914 but in 1704. So you have a lot to learn.

You may not call a soldier a bastard or an officer a bugger, as in either case it may be true.

Remember the word Bastard is a challenge to a fight. A man is a coward who does not take it up. It is a reflection on his mother.

While on the subject of swearing, the favourite word of the soldier designated by the sergeant giving evidence as F and the word spelt by the office boy with a K are not used amongst officers, or weren't in my day. *Tempora mutantur*.

There are two things you should never cast a doubt on or criticise – a man's sense of humour and his horsemanship. The less he has, the more he will resent it. Cast doubts on his general morality, his professional ability, or even his honesty and he will never mind, but the other two! No; never!

THE INFANTRYMAN AND THE HORSE

Every Englishman loves a horse as long as he can bet on it and does not have to look after it.

The horse is an animal which bites at one end and kicks at the other and is damned uncomfortable in the middle.

It has to have its hair brushed twice a day and resents it as much as the infantryman who has to do it.

A horse always seems to require attention when the infantryman most requires food and rest himself.

Except with regard to trotting, the cavalry feels the same about the horse, but for their very life daren't say so.

The horse is better than the mule; its kicks are easier to avoid and all horses don't bite.

FOR GUNNERS ONLY

Gunners are poor, proud and pious. Hear them praying at a mounted Battery drill, and you will have no doubt about the last. Three things only are sacred to them – his O.P. [Observation Post], his telephone wires and his wife.

This may account for the proverb, 'Almost as ugly as a Gunner's wife or a commissariat mule.'

It took three years to make an R.A. driver and fifteen years to turn out a battery commander, before the war proved that an intelligent civilian could be quite an efficient driver in three weeks or a battery commander in fifteen.

Note. At the end of the war any gunner subaltern with nine months' war service knew more about gunnery and shooting a battery than the average B.G.R.A. [Brigadier General Royal Artillery]. One B.G.R.A. in 1916 did not know at which end a howitzer was loaded. A fact.

The same maxim holds good in gunnery as in cards. One good look is worth all the calculation in the world.

Sappers are mad, married or Methodist. No task may be abandoned because of shell fire.

This they interpret to mean, draw the maximum fire possible on any task undertaken. Very heroic but it makes them, and trench mortars, very unpopular with their neighbours.

A Regimental Sergeant-Major is as near omnipotence as it is possible to be in this world. Only two people can question his actions. One is the C.O., who doesn't, the other, the Adjutant, who knows better.

Never buy a horse or a car from a brother officer unless you are rich enough not to resent being stung. For the same reason never sell one to a senior as rich or poor he will resent it.

SOCIAL

A Subaltern must not; a Captain may; a Major should; and a Colonel must marry.

You will never know as much as you (think you) do when you join, but remember even the newest joined subaltern is not always infallible.

Always forget that your C.O. has ever told you about his first tiger, or your Captain how he once won a Selling Plate at Aldershot.

> 'I heard some men talking about your shooting tiger in the Club, Sir. Is it true that—' Then his story with suitable embroidery of your own.
>
> 'Jack Anthony was telling some fellows about your riding at Aldershot.'
>
> 'My father asked me, were you the man, who, etc.'

Such phrases will get you a reputation for brains. This helps in the matter of leave.

About women, being under 21 you will know all about the sex, their mental processes and line of action under all and any circumstances. No need of advice from anyone. It takes ten years of married life to realise you don't know even one.

A dog in barracks is a misery to itself, a nuisance to its owner and causes more quarrels than a woman.

Keep clear of all quarrels, especially other people's. 'Blessed are the peacemakers for they shall inherit the kingdom of heaven' and damn soon too if they aren't careful.

Always agree with the man who is telling you about his row. He will then see that you are far more intelligent than he thought. If the other fellow asked what you meant by it, tell him you had not heard his side of it and of course he is in the right.

When anyone says, 'Now I really and truly want your advice.' He doesn't. He wants you to agree with what he has already made up his mind to do, so if it goes wrong, he has someone else to blame.

FINANCE AND GENERAL

Cultivate a reputation for generosity and poverty.

Pay for the first round of drinks while the circle is small. It always grows so you will get more drinks than you pay for.

Always have a spare bucket of gaspers to hand, thus you can smoke other people's Turkish.

Tip the man who gets the taxi. It will be the other man's turn to pay it.

When doing a show get the tickets, they cost less than the dinner.

Always lend your motorbike to the man whose car is in dock, thus he can't refuse you the loan of his car when your bike is out of action, which is easy, especially in bad weather.

Always fumble if you see any signs of the other man paying.

You are not 'broke' until the interest on the money you have borrowed exceeds your total income from all sources. Don't let this worry you, leave the worrying to the lender. You've had his money.

Never keep a woman, a racehorse, or a pack of hounds. Some other fool will always keep them for your enjoyment.

Always share with anyone who has more than yourself. This is true socialism.

ON THE STAFF

Any job is better than no job, even an A.D.C. to a Colonial Governor with five ugly daughters.

The Staff College is a close corporation. Their power only exists in the ignorance of the masses. Once it is known that anyone can become a successful general without passing through its sacred portals, its power will be gone. Any exception only got away with it by allowing the P.S.C.s [Passed Staff College] on their staffs to run the show without interference; so they tell you.

The chief attributes of a successful soldier are that he should come from a good public school (or wish he had), be a member of the Church of England, a crusted Tory, neat but not gaudy in dress, with no new opinions on anything. There are exceptions, who have risen by entirely contrary methods, but they only prove the rule. Think of all the generals and staff officers you know.

To get on you must be popular and never make an enemy. The man who never makes an enemy never makes anything else. If you get on you will make enemies. This is all very confusing but true.

The Staff deserve all the decorations they (earn) get in a war. They are a picked body of men; either for their brains or the beauty of their female relatives and must have some recompense for their loss of self-respect and sleepless nights. Someone is always trying to pinch their job. You may perhaps be the lucky one. No one is robbing you of sleep by trying to pinch your job in the trenches.

Once you have got on the Staff, hang on to the bottom of your velvet bottomed chair with both hands and keep one eye on the chair just above you and one on the boot of the man just below you. He is just as ready to give you a kick in the pants and pinch the chair above him as you are. (This applies more in war than in peace.) Any time left over can be devoted to your work.

Never miss an opportunity to crawl and toady to any general's wife you may meet. You never know how soon you may want another job.

Always be mysterious. It impresses the ignorant and hides your ignorance.

When you have made a thorough mess of a thing such phrases to the victims are useful:

'Of course there are reasons for all this but I cannot tell them.'

'You would understand if you knew the big idea at the back.'

'You can't make omelettes without breaking eggs.'

'The General wanted to see how you would act under adverse circumstances. He is very pleased with the way you got out of it.' This will stop him telling the General what he thinks of his staff.

When you get high up on the Staff, you can afford to be polite and even helpful to Mr. Bloody Regimental Fellow; occasionally.

Marry the relation of a high placed politician. To avoid having to support you himself, he will undertake the country does.

FINAL

Really the life in the Services is the best in the world, and your brother officers the best fellows in the British Empire, which, of course, includes the World and Eire, so don't believe a word of these Maxims; just act on them.

TO OFFICER CADETS AT
THE GERMAN SCHOOL OF ARTILLERY

A copy of this revealing document, which was printed in April 1943 – three months after Generalfeldmarschal Friedrich

Paulus's surrender at Stalingrad and just a month before the capture of Generaloberst Hans von Arnim in Tunisia – was found amongst the personal effects of a German officer taken prisoner by the Irish Guards shortly before the end of the Second World War:

BEHAVIOUR IN SOCIETY

1. Paying a Visit
    (a) Visiting hours: 1130–1300 hrs on Sundays, 1700–1800 hrs on weekdays. Never later, and never in the afternoon.
    (b) Visiting card must be of a plain and simple design. Unmarried officers should leave a separate card for the householder, his wife and each grown-up daughter.
    (c) Dress: SD jacket, long trousers, small type badges of rank, sword, stiff peaked cap and white gloves.
    (d) In the hall: remove cloak, but retain belt. Take sword and hat with you, and wear gloves.
    (e) Entering a room: carry hat in left hand. On taking a seat, lay the hat down.
    (f) Wearing gloves: when paying a visit, walking in street, or on official business, both gloves must always be worn. It is impolite when a superior officer stretches out his arm to shake hands, to keep him waiting while a glove is removed.
    (g) Coming and going:
        (1) Length of visit should be about ten minutes.
        (2) Do not look at your watch.
        (3) No reasons should be given for terminating the visit.
        (4) On leaving, do not turn your back on the company when opening the door.
    (h) Conversation: avoid any mention of your superiors in conversation. Relatives should be referred to as 'Herr Vater', 'Fräulein Schwester', etc. (i.e. never 'my wife').

2. Introductions

   When introducing two ladies to one another, use the phrase: 'May I make the ladies known to one another: Frau X – Frau Y'. The title of their husbands should be omitted (exception: 'Excellenz'). The hand of elderly married women should be kissed, but never in public.

3. Forms of address

   Unmarried women:

   (a) In general – 'Gnädiges Fräulein'.
   (b) Baroness – 'Gnädiges Fräulein'.
   (c) Countess – 'Gräfin, not Fräulein Gräfin' (Komtess in Southern Germany).

4. Entertainments

   (a) Wine: white wine to be drunk from tall glasses, red wine from short glasses.
   (b) Dances: first dance and quadrilles always with dinner partner. Never dance continually with one and the same lady. As a matter of principle, dance as soon as possible with the lady of the house and her daughters.
   (c) Flowers: never present with the paper round them. They should be unwrapped in the hall. In presenting flowers, hold the stalks downwards.

5. Written communications

   (a) Form of address: always choose the form of address to which the recipient is accustomed, and that which he has a right to expect from a well-bred young man, i.e. 'Hochverehrter Herr' or 'Hochzuverehrender Herr (plus title)'.
   (b) Contents of letter: must conform to H.Dv.30 para 8.
   (c) Ending: in finishing correspondence with officials or untitled persons, long conventional polite formulas should be avoided, and the phrase 'Heil Hitler' used.

GENERAL BEHAVIOUR

No flowers to be worn on uniforms or carried on vehicles. For troops returning to the Fatherland from campaigns, permission for the use of flowers may be obtained from Higher Authority. (Comment: GOC 7 Army please note.)

At the horse races, the officer himself must NOT approach the Totalisator. The theatre may NOT be visited in riding boots. It is forbidden for officers in uniform to take part in entertainment.

TO BRITISH SERVICEMEN IN FRANCE

From *Instructions for British Servicemen in France 1944*, prepared by the Political Warfare Executive, issued by the Foreign Office and republished by the Bodleian Library, Oxford, in 2005:

WOMEN – French women, both young and old, are far from shy and you will, if you are a man of sense, make them your friends. But do not mistake friendship for willingness to give you their favours. The same sort of girl with whom you can take liberties in England can be found in France, and the same sort of girl whom you would grossly offend in this country would be greatly offended if you were to 'try anything on' in France.

The fathers, brothers and fiancés of French girls will often be unable to protect them because they are fighting the Germans or have been deported to Germany. Apart from any question of discipline, you are on your honour to behave to their women-folk as you would wish them to behave to yours. If you do not, you will injure the reputation of the British soldier, by showing a worse example than the Germans, who at the start, at least, behaved with considerable restraint, though they later lapsed. As for the loose women, if you have noted the facts on page 7 about the prevalence of V.D., you will see good reasons for avoiding them.

—DO'S—

The French are our friends. The Germans are our enemies and the enemies of France. Remember that the Germans individually often behaved well in France. We have got to behave better.

We are helping to free France. Thousands of Frenchmen have been shot in France for keeping alive the spirit of freedom. Let the French know that you realize the great part Frenchmen have played, both in the last war and in this war.

The French are more polite than most of us. Remember to call them 'Monsieur, Madame, Mademoiselle', not just 'Oy!'

Be patient if you find a Frenchman hard to understand – he is having difficulties too.

Remember to salute a French civilian or policeman when you address them. This is a normal form of politeness practised by the French. Salute when entering and leaving a private house, a café, or a shop.

Be natural, but don't make yourself too much at home till you are sure your French friends like it. Remember the intense suffering of the French since 1940. Make allowances for this.

—DON'TS—

Don't criticize the French Army's defeat of 1940. Many Frenchmen are convinced that they had a fine but insufficiently equipped army, not very well led. Many others are themselves critical of the French Army of 1940, but they, too, will resent their own criticism coming from a foreigner.

Don't get into arguments about religion or politics. If a Frenchman raises one of the points which have strained Anglo-French relations since 1940, drop the matter. There are two sides to every question, but you don't want to take either.

Don't get drawn into discussions about the comparative merits and successes of the United Nations.

Don't, even if food is offered to you, eat the French out of house and home. If you do, someone may starve.

Don't mess things up even in an empty billet. Someone will live there after you.

Don't drink yourself silly. If you get the chance to drink wine, learn to 'take it'. The failure of some British troops to do so was the one point made against our men in France in 1939–40 and again in North Africa.

Don't sell or give away your food or equipment.

TO AMERICAN SERVICEMEN IN BRITAIN

From *Instructions for American Servicemen in Britain 1942*, issued by War Department, Washington, DC, and republished by the Bodleian Library, Oxford, in 2004:

SOME IMPORTANT DO'S AND DON'TS

BE FRIENDLY – but don't intrude anywhere it seems you are not wanted.

You will find the British money system easier than you think. A little study beforehand on shipboard will make it still easier.

You are higher paid than the British 'Tommy'. Don't rub it in. Play fair with him. He can be a pal in need.

Don't show off or brag or bluster – 'swank' as the British say. If somebody looks in your direction and says, 'He's chucking his weight about,' you can be pretty sure you're off base. That's the time to pull in your ears.

If you are invited to eat with a family don't eat too much. Otherwise you may eat up their weekly rations.

Don't make fun of British speech or accents. You sound just as funny to them but they will be too polite to show it.

Avoid comments on the British Government or politics.

Don't try to tell the British that America won the last war or make wise-cracks about the war debts or about British defeats in this war.

NEVER criticize the King or Queen.

Don't criticize the food, beer, or cigarettes to the British. Remember they have been at war since 1939.

TO LAND GIRLS

With German U-boats threatening Britain's vital trade routes and Europe under Nazi control, there was a push towards self-sufficiency in food production during the Second World War. Encouraged by slogans such as 'For a healthy, happy job', 'We could do with thousands more like you …' and 'Reap the harvest of victory', many young women answered the clarion call to join the Women's Land Army. Numbers peaked at 65,000 in the summer of 1943 – with an average of a thousand joining every week – just as the Battle of the Atlantic drew to a successful conclusion. In order to encourage them in 'making the most of the country', Dr Wilfred Shewell-Cooper, Principal of the Horticultural Training Centre and Superintendent of Swanley Horticultural College for Women, offered the following advice, published in *Land Girl: A Manual for Volunteers in the Women's Land Army 1941* (English Universities Press, 1941, reprinted by Amberley (Stroud), 2011):

The town girl does not always find it easy to live in the country. She naturally misses all the amenities that she is used to. She cannot pop in to the local cinema when she feels inclined. She cannot even go round to the local fish-and-chip shop or to a snack bar if she wants a quick meal in the evening. She is not able to stroll down the High Street and have a look at the shops and see the latest fashions, and there are not, of course, the number of men about to go to dances with at the local Palais de Dance.

Some townspeople are apt to look upon all country folk as country bumpkins. They have an idea that it is only the town folk who know anything, and because people in the country are not so slick, or are not so well dressed, or perhaps are not up to the latest fashion, they are apt to be labelled as old-fashioned, and rather a back number.

Actually, country folk usually know far more than those who are bred and born in towns and cities. They may not know all the names of the film stars and the pictures in which they have appeared, but they do know the names of the birds and their habits. They are able to tell whether it is going to be wet or fine the next day. They know which herbs are useful and all about the ways of wild animals. They have a different kind of knowledge, that is all.

The Land Army volunteer, therefore, who is going to work on a farm and live in a village must be prepared to see the 'other fellow's' point of view. She will never be a success if she goes into her new surroundings determined to show them a thing or two. She will only be stared at if she wears her very latest Bond Street creation at the local social or 'hop'. She will be considered rude if she is continually saying, 'Fancy you not knowing that', or is constantly boasting of her doings in the town.

It does need a little effort at first to fit in with new surroundings. It is always necessary to consider the farmer and his family;

to consider the billeter, and to remember to help in the little things, and to lend a hand sometimes without being asked.

There are so many obvious things which get forgotten. The volunteer should always be punctual in her hours; she should not smoke about the place, especially in farm buildings; she should shut gates behind her; she should put tools back properly, so that the next person who wants them can find them; she should never leave a job half done just because she finds it difficult.

A farmer is not made in a month, and, after training, some girls are inclined to try to teach the farmer his business, often with unfortunate results. So if a volunteer has been taught a method different from the farmer's, she should always ask his permission before making the change. Farmers have no time to bother with fussy volunteers. They expect girls who have offered to do the work to carry it out without complaint.

TRYING IT OUT

A volunteer who enrols to 'see if she likes it' is a liability, not an asset. However patriotic she may feel, she does not help her country by enrolling in the Land Army unless she is certain she can stay the course.

It is quite a good plan to try carrying buckets full of water for half an hour or more at a time, and then attempting to pitch earth onto a barrow and then onto a shelf about breast high for another hour or so, to see whether she can bear the aches and pains entailed. Farming work is not spectacular, but it does mean hard physical strain, but any girl who can endure it finds compensation in the knowledge that she is playing a very important part in National Service.

DISSATISFACTION

Some farm jobs are monotonous, but they are essential to food production. The volunteer should do them thoroughly and systematically, for by putting her best into the work she will make it interesting.

If, however, she is not completely happy, or is dissatisfied in any way, she should not throw up her job hastily, or grumble to her fellow-workers. The matter should be taken to the farmer himself, the County Secretary consulted or the District Representative talked to, and in this way it is usually possible to get matters put right.

MAKE-UP

Town girls on the whole use far more make-up than country girls. The Women's Land Army volunteer should therefore be prepared to 'tone down' her lips, complexions and nails considerably.

A certain amount of make-up may be used at parties and local village dances, but long nails are quite unsuited to work on a farm, especially when covered with bright crimson nail-varnish.

The volunteer will soon find that, as the other girls from the village do not use make-up, she will prefer not to use it herself, so as not to look conspicuous. She will find, too, that she will get such a healthy colour to her cheeks that rouging will not be necessary!

LENDING A HAND

Be prepared to do some useful work in the village during your spare time. It may be that you can get into touch with the local representative of the W.V.S. and do some knitting. Perhaps you will be able to help by forming one of the personnel of the village First-Aid Point. You can be very useful, too, by putting your name down as one of the fire-watchers.

Some Land Army volunteers have taken on definite voluntary jobs in the village. At least one is organising the local branch of the County Library, and is very much liked and appreciated as a result.

SOCIALS

Join the local Women's Institute, and go to their meetings if they are held at a convenient time. Go to any socials there may be in the village, and try to fit in naturally. Don't push yourself, and so spoil things. Take part in all such activities in a humble manner, and help to break down any prejudice there may be against women on the land. Each volunteer can do her part to ensure smooth working and to help in securing the good name of the Women's Land Army.

MAIDS

When living at a farm where a maid is kept, the volunteer should remember that she also is employed by the farmer, and not by herself. She should not, therefore, expect the maid to wait on her, nor should she give the maid extra work and extra bother.

STICKING TO IT

The Land Army is judged by its members. A good volunteer is a good advertisement.

Every volunteer should remember that money has been spent on her equipment and training, to make her a *specialist* for a vital job. She should not, therefore, *ever drop out*. She must feel that *she* is feeding the nation. If she drops out, someone may starve.

Further, wherever a recruit or a full Women's Land Army volunteer gives up, she represents a dead loss to her country, and her country cannot afford dead losses in a war like this.

There is the example to think of, too. If one volunteer gives up, it has an effect on others. Recruits coming along get to know, and so 'rot' may set in.

The Land Army must have a motto – 'Stick to It.'

Girls who had to resign in the early days of the war for a good reason, or just to change their jobs, or even to go home, are wanted – they should, therefore, if reliable, offer their services once more, for they are certainly needed.

Training given at the Government's expense will thus *not* be wasted, nor will the experience gained be lost.

ON THE WEARING OF BOWLER HATS IN THE 1980s

As a trustee of his regiment, Ashe Windham very kindly obtained for me a copy of *Irish Guards: Notes for Officers 2013*, of which I would never have known otherwise. I was delighted to read that, on 3 August 1979, the Regimental Adjutant of The Irish Guards, Major Willie (now Sir William) Mahon, wrote a letter to all the officers in the regiment:

Officers wearing bowler hats in London have been objects of ridicule in the eyes of tourists and the general population for some time. This applies especially to younger Officers. 1980 is almost upon us and we must move with the times while preserving standards.

It has therefore been decided to discontinue the rule whereby Officers were expected to appear at Guard Mounting from Horse Guards, at Regimental Headquarters or in Headquarters London District dressed in a bowler hat.

Officers who wish to wear a bowler hat are free to do so, but it should be clearly understood that because a senior or older Officer wears a bowler hat there is NO obligation on younger Officers to do so.

All Officers are expected to wear a hat in London and hats should be of a restrained and sober pattern without unduly wide brims or broad ribbons. Officers sporting Tyrolean ropes, shaving brushes, feathers or other extravagant decorations in their hats will incur the wrath of the Regimental Lieutenant Colonel.

For the Annual March to the Guards Memorial Officers are under no obligation to wear bowler hats.

There will be no need for any Officer to buy a bowler hat in the future unless he wishes to do so.

It was only a matter of days before Nigel Dempster, the diarist at *The Daily Mail*, seized upon – and sent up – this eminently sensible guidance. Major Willie Mahon was following a long tradition within the Household Division. For example, on 10 December 1813, as the Peninsular War was drawing to a close, Lord Arthur Hill wrote a memorandum at Bayonne to the officers of the Grenadier Guards: 'Lord Wellington does not approve the use of umbrellas during enemy's firing, and will not allow the "gentlemen's sons" to make themselves ridiculous in the eyes of the enemy.'

In Their Own Words

This field of study is so enormous that I have limited myself to a selection of military quotations, focusing on eternal verities and solid advice, sometimes with just a touch of humour. The military quotations are then followed by some succinct phrases, either spoken or written by some of the most influential political or military leaders during the major wars of the twentieth century.

MILITARY QUOTATIONS

Sun Tzu, author of *The Art of War*, who is thought to have lived between 544 and 496 BC, offers some eminently practical advice:

> The supreme art of war is to subdue the enemy without fighting … If you know the enemy and know yourself, you need not fear the result of a hundred battles. If you know yourself but not the enemy, for every victory gained you will also suffer a defeat. If you know neither the enemy nor yourself, you will succumb in every battle … Appear weak when you are strong, and strong when you are weak.

In Book IX of his *History of Rome*, Titus Livius Patavinus, who was more commonly known as Livy, wrote that 'valour is the soldier's adornment'. Queen Victoria may perhaps have been familiar with Livy's writings since she wrote to Lord Panmure, Secretary of State for War, on 7 January 1856: 'The Queen returns the drawings for the "Victoria Cross". She has marked the one she approves with an X; she thinks, however, that it might be a trifle smaller. The motto would be better "For Valour" than "For the Brave," as this would lead to the inference that only those are deemed brave who have got the Victoria Cross.'

The fourth century AD writer Publius Flavius Vegetius Renatus, commonly known as Vegetius, was the author of *Rei militaris instituta*, also known as *Epitoma rei militaris*, an influential text in the Middle Ages. His most famous aphorism was:

'Qui desiderat pacem, praeparet bellum' or, in translation, 'Let him who desires peace prepare for war.'

On 10 April 1778, the great Dr Samuel Johnson said to his amanuensis, James Boswell: 'Every man thinks meanly of himself for not having been a soldier, or not having been at sea.'

In Book I of *Vom Kriege* (published by Dümmlers Verlag: Berlin, 1832), or *On War* (published in translation London: N. Trübner & Co. 1873), the Prussian general, Carl von Clausewitz (1780–1831) wrote: 'We see, therefore, that war is not merely an act of policy but a true political instrument, a continuation of political intercourse carried on with other means.' Later in the same volume, he wrote that 'if the mind is to emerge unscathed from this relentless struggle with the unforeseen, two qualities are indispensable: first, an intellect that, even in the darkest hour, retains some glimmerings of the inner light which leads to truth; and second, the courage to follow this faint light wherever it may lead.' In *On War*, Clausewitz also observed that 'this difficulty of seeing things correctly, which is one of the greatest sources of friction in War, makes things appear quite different from what was expected.'

Field Marshal Arthur Wellesley, 1st Duke of Wellington, Commander-in-Chief of the British Army 1827–52, shared Clausewitz's concerns when he pointed out that 'all the business of war, and indeed all the business of life, is to endeavour to find out what you don't know by what you do; that's what

I called "guessing what was at the other side of the hill".' On reviewing a draft sent to join him in Portugal in 1809, he reputedly said: 'I don't know what effect these men will have upon the enemy, but, by God, they terrify me.' In conversation with Philip Stanhope on 11 November 1831, the Duke said:

> A French army is composed very differently from ours. The conscription calls out a share of every class – no matter whether your son or my son – all must march; but our friends – I may say it in this room – are the very scum of the earth. People talk about enlisting from their fine military feeling – all stuff – no such thing. Some of our men enlist from having got bastard children – some for minor offences – many more for drink; but you can hardly conceive such a set brought together, and it is really wonderful that we should have made them the fine fellows they are.[1]

On 7 February 1821, George Gordon, 6th Baron Byron, wrote to his publisher, John Murray: 'What makes a regiment of soldiers a more noble object of view than the same mass of mob? Their arms, their dresses, their banners, and the art and artificial symmetry of their position and movements.' In 1823, while living in Genoa, Byron succumbed to requests that he might involve himself in the War of Independence that the Greeks were fighting against their Ottoman overlords. Before sailing with an expedition to seize Lepanto, however, he died from disease at Missolonghi on 19 April 1824.

---

[1] Philip Henry Stanhope, *Notes on Conversations with the Duke of Wellington*, London: privately published, 1886.

On 6 March 1856, Florence Nightingale wrote from Barrack Hospital, Scutari, to Lieutenant Colonel John Henry Lefroy:

I have never been able to join in the popular cry about the reck-lessness, sensuality, helplessness of the soldier. On the contrary I should say (and no woman perhaps has ever seen more of the manufacturing and agricultural classes of England than I have – before I came out here) that I have never seen so teachable and helpful a class as the Army generally. Give them opportunity promptly and securely to send money home – and they will use it. Give them schools and lectures and they will come to them. Give them books and a game and a Magic Lanthorn and they will leave off drinking. Give them suffering and they will bear it. Give them work and they will do it. I had rather have to do

with the Army generally than with any other class I have ever attempted to serve.

Sir John Lefroy later became Inspector General of Army Schools.

The seemingly never-ending series of military campaigns in India during the nineteenth century provided *Punch* with material for what Richard Holmes describes as 'the two great Latin jokes of British India'. The following lines were printed on page 141 of Volume XXX of *Punch*, published on 22 March 1856, little more than a year before the outbreak of the Indian Mutiny and soon after the Governor General, Lord Dalhousie, had annexed Oudh:

> *'Peccavi – I've sinned' wrote Lord Ellen so proud.*
> *More briefly Dalhousie wrote – 'Vovi – I've Oude'.*

After Lieutenant General Sir Colin Campbell had success-fully relieved Lucknow, after the second siege, one of his well-educated and witty staff officers is supposed to have said: '*Nunc fortunatus sum*' or 'I am in luck now', with the result that there were really three 'great Latin jokes'.

Major General Sir Henry Havelock, who died just a week after Campbell's arrival at Lucknow, observed that 'war is not a romance, but always a matter of nice calculation, of fluctuat-ing chances.'

The old schoolboy joke is that President Abraham Lincoln drafted the Gettysburg Address while travelling to Gettysburg on the back of an envelope; in fact he went by train from Washington. There are, however, a few unusual aspects of the Dedication of the National Cemetery at Gettysburg on 19 November 1863. The main speaker was Edward Everett, a past president of Harvard College and former Secretary of State, who spoke for almost two hours. As President, Abraham Lincoln had been asked to make a 'few appropriate remarks', which he duly did:

> Fourscore and seven years ago our fathers brought forth upon this continent a new nation, conceived in liberty, and dedicated to the proposition that all men are created equal. Now we are engaged in a great civil war, testing whether that nation, or any nation so conceived and so dedicated, can long endure. We are met on a great battlefield of that war. We have come to dedicate a portion of that field as a final resting-place of those who here gave their lives that that nation might live. It is altogether fitting and proper that we should do this. But in a larger sense we cannot dedicate, we cannot consecrate, we cannot hallow this ground. The brave men, living and dead, who struggled here, have consecrated it far above our power to add or detract. The world will little note, nor long remember, what we say here, but it can never forget what they did here. It is for us, the living, rather to be dedicated here to the unfinished work they have thus far so nobly advanced. It is rather for us to be here dedicated to the great task remaining before us, that from these honored dead we take increased devotion to that cause for which they here gave the last full measure of devotion; that we here highly resolve that the dead shall not have died in vain, that this nation, under God, shall have a new birth of freedom; and that the government of the people, by the people, and for the people, shall not perish from the earth.

In respect of memory, Lincoln was both right and wrong. While no one now recalls a single word of Everett's oration, Lincoln's carefully chosen and well-modulated 264 words – redolent of the King James version of the Bible – seared themselves into the soul of the nation and soon became compulsory learning for schoolchildren in the United States. Perhaps some of them resented it so much that they had to have their little joke.

The Confederate general, James Longstreet, was known to General Robert E. Lee as his 'Old War Horse'; however, he was later blamed, rather unfairly, for the defeat at Gettysburg, when he attacked rather later than Lee had ordered him to attack, but after he had successfully concentrated the bulk of his force. In 1902 Longstreet said at a Memorial Day Parade: 'I hope to live long enough to see my surviving comrades march side by side with the Union veterans along Pennsylvania Avenue, and then I will die happy.' Sadly, that never happened, since James Longstreet died on 2 January 1904, in his eighty-third year, having outlived most of his critics.

The Russo-Turkish War 1877–8 came about as a direct consequence of Russian attempts to profit from the decline of the so-called 'Sick Man of Europe', the Ottoman Empire, following a series of risings against Turkish rule in the Balkans. After Herzegovina, then Bulgaria, and finally Serbia and Montenegro all rebelled against their Turkish rulers, Russia intervened, but only having been assured of the neutrality of Austria-Hungary. The response of the British prime minister, Benjamin Disraeli, was to order the Mediterranean Fleet to Constantinople, in order to support the Turks, who had been our allies during the Crimean War, little more than twenty years earlier. It was a successful intervention. The word 'jingoism' derives from a music hall song written by G. W. Hunt in 1878:

We don't want to fight, but by Jingo if we do,
We've got the ships, we've got the men, and got the money too.
We've fought the Bear before, and while we're Britons true,
The Russians shall not have Constantinople.

In a speech delivered in Columbus, Ohio, on 11 August 1880, General William Tecumseh Sherman said: 'There is many a boy here today who looks on war as all glory, but, boys, it is all hell.'

In Act III of *The Devil's Disciple* (1897), George Bernard Shaw has a character declaim: 'The British soldier can stand up to anything except the British War Office.'

The famous words of Georges Benjamin Clemenceau, prime minister of France 1906–9 and 1917–20 – 'War is far too important to be left to the generals' – were spoken by Brigadier General Jack D. Ripper, commander of Burpleson Air Force Base, in the cult anti-nuclear war film, *Dr. Strangelove or: How I Learned to Stop Worrying and Love the Bomb* (1964).

In *John Bull's Other Island*, first produced in 1904, one of George Bernard Shaw's characters said: 'There are only two qualities in the world: efficiency and inefficiency; and only two sorts of people: the efficient and the inefficient.' General Baron Kurt von Hammerstein-Equord, Commander-in-Chief, German Reichswehr 1930–4, and an ardent opponent of Adolf Hitler, may possibly have had Shaw in mind when he wrote:

> I divide my officers into four classes as follows: the clever, the industrious, the lazy and the stupid. Each officer always possesses two of these classes. Those who are clever and industrious I appoint to the General Staff. Use can under certain circumstances be made of those who are stupid and lazy. The man who is clever and lazy qualifies for the highest leadership posts. He has the requisite nerves and the mental clarity for difficult decisions. He who is stupid and industrious must be got rid of. He is too dangerous.[2]

In 1940 General Sir Archibald Wavell said to Brigadier Eric Dorman-Smith, who developed the plan for Operation Compass, as a result of which Italian forces were driven out of western Egypt and eastern Libya: 'A little unorthodoxy is a dangerous thing – but without it one seldom wins battles.' Rommel wrote of Wavell that he was 'the only one who showed a touch of genius'.

The charismatic – if frequently controversial – American general, George S. Patton, once said: 'If we take the generally accepted definition of bravery as a quality which knows no fear, I have never seen a brave man. All men are frightened. The more intelligent they are, the more they are frightened.'

---

[2] A. P. W. (Wavell), *Notes and Ideas 1939–46*.

He is also quoted as saying: 'We herd sheep, we drive cattle, we lead people. Lead me, follow me, or get out of my way.' As far as leadership is concerned, Field Marshal Viscount Slim wrote: 'There are no bad regiments, there are only bad officers.'

General Sir Gordon MacMillan of MacMillan and Knap commanded 15th (Scottish) Infantry Division in Normandy, 49th (West Riding) Infantry Division in Holland and Germany and 51st (Highland) Infantry Division in the closing stages of the Second World War, culminating in the Victory Parade in Bremerhaven on 12 May 1945. In a reassuringly practical preface to a wartime training directive, he wrote that

> a soldier on the battlefield, beset by fear and doubt, is far more in need of a guide to action than any games player at Lords or Wimbledon. Better to know instinctively some orthodox line of conduct than to be paralysed by the uncertainty of what to do. Let us, therefore, study and draw up some lines of conduct – simple guides for the simple soldier – so that we may ensure that our soldiers, when faced with problems on the battlefield, will have an answer to them.

On Thursday 22 December 1944, during the Battle of the Bulge, General Heinrich von Lüttwitz of XLVII Panzer Corps sent four emissaries to deliver a message inviting surrender 'To the USA Commander of the encircled town of Bastogne'. Having reached the American lines at 11.30 a.m., they were blindfolded and taken to the command post of 327th Infantry Company. The message was then delivered to the acting Divisional Chief of Staff, Lieutenant Colonel Ned Moore, who duly informed Brigadier General Tony McAuliffe, acting Divisional Commander. The Germans insisted on a written reply and that from Brigadier General McAuliffe has since passed into legend, as well as being the shortest entry in *The Oxford Dictionary of Quotations*: 'Nuts!' Somewhat puzzled, the leading German spokesman asked: 'Is the reply negative or affirmative?' In Bastogne the Historical Center is known affectionately as Nuts Museum, there is a Nuts Café serving Nuts Salade while many of the shops in the town sell merchandise – T-shirts and coffee mugs, etc. – emblazoned with the word 'Nuts'.

On 19 April 1951, General of the Army Douglas MacArthur addressed a Joint Meeting of the US Congress:

> In war there can be no substitute for victory … I am closing my 52 years of military service. When I joined the army, even before the turn of the century, it was the fulfillment of all my boyish hopes and dreams. The world has turned over many times since I took the oath on the plain at West Point, and the hopes and dreams have all since vanished, but I still remember the refrain of one of the most popular barracks ballads of that day which proclaimed most proudly that old soldiers never die; they just fade away. And like the old soldier of that ballad, I now close my military career and just fade away, an old soldier who tried to do his duty as God gave him the light to see that duty. Good Bye.

In January 1957, Charlton Ogburn's story, 'Merrill's Marauders', was published in *Harper's Magazine*. Ogburn recounted his first-hand experiences of the campaign in Burma during the Second World War, including this memorable – and much-quoted – passage:

> We trained hard, but it seemed that every time we were beginning to form up into teams we would be reorganized. Presumably the plans for our employment were being changed. I was to learn later in life that, perhaps because we are so good at organizing, we tend as a nation to meet any new situation by *re*organizing; and a wonderful method it can be for creating the illusion of progress while producing confusion, inefficiency and demoralization.

In Kuwait on 19 March 2003, Lieutenant Colonel Tim Collins, commanding the 1st Battalion, The Royal Irish Regiment, gave an uplifting speech to his men on the eve of battle:

> We go to Iraq to liberate not to conquer. We will not fly our flags in their country. We are entering Iraq to free a people and the only flag which will be flown in that ancient land is their own. Show respect for them … Iraq is steeped in history. It is the site of the Garden of Eden, of the Great Flood and the birthplace of Abraham. Tread lightly there. You will see things that no man could pay to see and you will have to go a long way to find a more decent, generous and upright people than the Iraqis. You will be embarrassed by their hospitality even though they have nothing. Don't treat them as refugees for they are in their own country. Their children will be poor, in years to come they will know that the light of liberation in their lives was brought by you. If there are casualties of war then remember that when they woke up and got dressed in the morning they did not plan to die this day. Allow them dignity in death. Bury them properly and mark their graves … As for ourselves, let's bring everyone

home and leave Iraq a better place for us having been there.
Our business now is north.

TWENTIETH-CENTURY WORDS ON WAR

The first five decades of the twentieth century – and the major
wars that they encompassed – may usefully be summarised in
the words that follow, all of which were either spoken or written
by influential participants.

On 14 June 1901, Sir Henry Campbell-Bannerman,
the Leader of the Liberal Party – and thus Leader of the
Opposition – who became prime minister four years later, gave
an impassioned speech at the National Reform Union about
British behaviour during the Second Anglo-Boer War, with
particular reference to the burning of farms and homesteads
and the introduction of so-called 'concentration camps': 'When
was a war not a war?   When it was carried on by methods of
barbarism.'

Ten years later, on 21 July 1911, in his annual speech at the
Mansion House, the Chancellor of the Exchequer, David Lloyd
George, wartime prime minister from late 1916, strayed off his
brief when he said:

> I am also bound to say this – that I believe it is essential, in the
> highest interests, not merely of this country, but of the world,
> that Britain should at all hazards maintain her place and her
> prestige amongst the Great Powers of the world. Her potent
> influence has many a time been in the past, and may yet be
> in the future, invaluable in the cause of human liberty. It has

more than once in the past redeemed continental nations, who are sometimes apt to forget that service, from overwhelming disaster, and even from national extinction.

In the House of Commons on 27 November 1911, Andrew Bonar Law, the Leader of the Conservative Party, who had become Leader of the Opposition just two weeks earlier, and who succeeded Lloyd George as prime minister in 1922, gave a perceptive speech in which he said: 'If, therefore, war should ever come between these two countries [Great Britain and Germany], which Heaven forbid! it will not, I think, be due to irresistible natural laws, it will be due to the want of human wisdom.' He repeated these words, almost verbatim, in the House of Commons on 6 August 1914.

Sir Edward Grey, later 1st Viscount Grey of Fallodon, who was Foreign Secretary for exactly eleven years, the longest continuous tenure in that office, first in Sir Henry Campbell-Bannerman's administration and later in that of Henry Herbert Asquith, said, presciently, on 3 August 1914: 'The lamps are going out all over Europe; we shall not see them lit again in our lifetime.' He died on 7 September 1933, the same year that Adolf Hitler became Chancellor of Germany.

On 4 August 1914, Theobald von Bethmann Hollweg, who served as Chancellor of Germany from 1909 to 1917, said to Sir Edward Goschen, the British Ambassador in Berlin: 'Just for a word – "neutrality", a word which in wartime has so often

been disregarded, just for a scrap of paper – Great Britain is going to make war.' The same words – at once cynical and incredulous – were immediately sent by despatch to the Foreign Office in London. Great Britain declared war at midnight on 4 August 1914.

Field Marshal Horatio Herbert, 1st Earl Kitchener of Khartoum, former Sirdar of the Egyptian Army, victor of the Battle of Omdurman in 1898 and Commander-in-Chief during the Second Anglo-Boer War, was appointed Secretary of State for War on the outbreak of the First World War.

His 'message to the soldiers of the British Expeditionary Force, 1914' was intended to be retained by each soldier in his pay-book:

> You are ordered abroad as a soldier of the King to help our French comrades against the invasion of a common enemy. You have to perform a task which will need your courage, your energy, your patience. Remember that the honour of the British Army depends on your individual conduct. It will be your duty not only to set an example of discipline and perfect steadfast-ness under fire but also to maintain the most friendly relations with those whom you are helping in this struggle. In this new experience you may find temptations both in wine and women. You must entirely resist both temptations, and, while treating all women with perfect courtesy, you should avoid any intimacy. Do your duty bravely. Fear God. Honour the King.

On 12 August 1914, King George V sent a message to the British Expeditionary Force, as they boarded their transports, bound for France and Flanders:

> You are leaving home to fight for the safety and honour of my Empire. Belgium, whose country we are pledged to defend, has been attacked and France is about to be invaded by the same powerful foe. I have implicit confidence in you my soldiers. Duty is your watchword, and I know your duty will be nobly done. I shall follow your every movement with deepest interest and mark with eager satisfaction your daily progress, indeed your welfare will never be absent from my thoughts. I pray God to bless you and guard you and bring you back victorious.

At Aix on 19 August 1914, Queen Victoria's eldest grandson, Kaiser Wilhelm II, issued an *Army Order*, which included these words: 'Exterminate the treacherous English, and walk over General French's contemptible little army.'

In early September 1914, only a week after taking command of the newly formed French Ninth Army, Général Ferdinand Foch is reputed to have said, at a critical juncture of the First Battle of the Marne: 'Mon centre cède, ma droite recule, situation excellente. J'attaque!' or, in translation, 'My centre is giving way, my right is in retreat, situation excellent. I shall attack.' Foch was later appointed Supreme Commander of the Allied Armies on the Western Front, leading them to victory in November 1918.

On 21 September 1914, *The Times* printed Laurence Binyon's poem, 'For the Fallen', the second verse of which now forms the central commemorative element of the traditional Service of Remembrance:

They shall grow not old, as we that are left grow old:
Age shall not weary them, nor the years condemn.
At the going down of the sun and in the morning
We will remember them.

Aged forty-five when he wrote 'For the Fallen', Laurence Binyon was then working at the British Museum. The following year, he volunteered to work as an orderly at a British hospital for French soldiers, Hôpital Temporaire d'Arc-en-Barrois.

Some confusion surrounds the next quotation. At the start of the Battle of Verdun in February 1916, Général Philippe Pétain was commanding the Second Army, in which command he was succeeded by Général Robert Nivelle, when he was promoted to command Army Group Centre. Such was the importance of the heavily fortified city of Verdun as a symbol of French resistance that these words, apparently first spoken by Nivelle, but often attributed to Pétain, have become famous: 'Ils ne passeront pas' or, in translation, 'They shall not pass.'

It is often said that only one Briton could have lost the First World War in a day: Admiral Sir John Jellicoe, who took command of the newly formed Grand Fleet on 4 August 1914. His day – which actually lasted from 31 May to 1 June 1916 – was the Battle of Jutland. The battle started disastrously for Vice-Admiral Sir David Beatty's Battlecruiser Squadron when two of his ships, HMS *Indefatigable* and HMS *Queen Mary*, exploded within less than half-an-hour of one another, leaving just twenty-two survivors from a combined crew of 2,283 officers and men. Beatty turned to his Flag-Captain, Ernle Chatfield, and said: 'There's something wrong with our bloody ships today, Chatfield.' Jellicoe, Beatty and Chatfield all served as First Sea Lord and were later ennobled.

The surrender of Russia and the resulting Treaty of Brest-Litovsk enabled Germany to move fifty divisions from the Eastern to the Western Fronts, for a final attempt at a breakthrough, before the arrival of American 'doughboys' shifted the balance inexorably against them. On 21 March 1918, Operation Michael, the first phase of the so-called *Kaiserschlacht*, took the British by surprise, as new tactics and sheer weight of numbers helped the Germans advance by up to forty miles over the old Somme battlefield in just two weeks. The next stage, Operation Georgette, which began on 9 April, took place further north, in the area of the River Lys. The resulting threat to the Channel ports was sufficiently serious for Field Marshal Sir Douglas Haig, Commander-in-Chief of the British Armies in France, to issue a Special Order of the Day on 11 April, closing with the following words: 'Every position must be held to the last man: there must be no retirement. With our backs to the wall, and believing in the justice of our cause, each one of us must fight on to the end. The safety of our homes and the Freedom of mankind alike depend upon the conduct of each one of us at this critical moment.'

On 10 December 1918, Sir Eric Geddes, Conservative Member of Parliament for Cambridge and First Lord of the Admiralty, albeit only for another month, delivered a speech at the Guildhall, Cambridge, in which he said: 'We will get everything out of her [Germany] that you can squeeze out of a lemon and a bit more ... I will squeeze her until you can hear the pips squeak.' These few words were a harbinger of what was to follow at the Treaty of Versailles, by which Germany felt so impoverished and ill-used that the seeds of the Second World War were sown. Sir Eric Geddes was equally hard on his own side: his chairmanship of the Committee on National

Expenditure led to such harsh cut-backs that it became known as 'the Geddes axe'.

It was a reflection of such cut-backs that a paper on Imperial Defence, published on 22 June 1926, concluded, rather astonishingly, that: 'The size of the forces of the Crown maintained by Great Britain is governed by various conditions peculiar to each service, and is not arrived at by any calculations of the requirements of foreign policy, nor is it possible that they should ever be so calculated.'

Frank Billings Kellogg, the US Secretary of State, was co-sponsor of the Kellogg-Briand Pact, signed in Paris on 27 August 1928:

> The high contracting parties solemnly declare in the names of their respective peoples that they condemn recourse to war for the solution of international controversies, and renounce it as an instrument of national policy in their relations with one another. The high contracting parties agree that the settlement or solution of all disputes or conflicts of whatever nature or of whatever origin they may be, which may rise among them, shall never be sought except by pacific means.

Slightly ironically, in the light of what occurred a decade later, Kellogg was awarded the Nobel Peace Prize in 1929.

At Berlin's Sportpalast on 26 September 1938 – little more than six months after the annexation of Austria – Adolf Hitler said,

in an impassioned speech: 'My patience is now at an end …
It is the last territorial claim which I have to make in Europe.'
The Munich Pact, which ceded to Germany the Sudetenland
region of Czechoslovakia, in which many ethnic Germans lived,
was signed just three days later.

On 3 September 1939, the day that Great Britain declared war
on Nazi Germany, two days after Poland had been invaded,
President Franklin Delano Roosevelt warned, in one of his regular 'fireside chats': 'When peace has been broken anywhere,
the peace of all countries everywhere is in danger.'

On 13 May 1940, three days after he had succeeded Neville
Chamberlain as prime minister, Winston Churchill said in the
House of Commons:

> I would say to the House as I said to those who have joined this
> government: I have nothing to offer but blood, toil, tears and
> sweat. We have before us an ordeal of the most grievous kind.
> We have before us many, many long months of struggle and of
> suffering. You ask, what is our aim? I can answer in one word:
> Victory. Victory at all costs – victory in spite of all terror – victory,
> however long and hard the road may be, for without victory
> there is no survival.

In a speech delivered at Westminster College, Fulton, Missouri,
on 5 March 1946, Winston Churchill, by then Leader of the
Opposition, said:

From Stettin in the Baltic to Trieste in the Adriatic an 'Iron Curtain' has descended across the Continent. Behind that line lie all the capitals of Central and Eastern Europe, Warsaw, Berlin, Prague, Vienna, Budapest, Belgrade, Bucharest and Sofia; all these famous cities and the populations around them lie in what I must call the Soviet sphere, and all are subject, in one form or another not only to Soviet influence but to a very high, and in some cases increasing, measure of control from Moscow.

The Cold War had begun.

Music and Songs

Morale is of crucial importance and, as Sir Garnet Wolseley acknowledged on page 201 of *The Soldier's Pocket-Book for Field Service*, music played a vital role:

> Whenever it is possible, have music to march to. If the band is broken up [their function during wartime is to act as stretcher-bearers], the drums and bugles should play together as the French do. Nothing is more martial in sound, and the men march a hundred per cent better to it than in silence. If you have nothing else, get your men to sing by companies. During long night marches in India at the beginning of the mutiny, I found that with singing we got on admirably, whilst, when we marched in silence, as men will do after the first half mile at night, they almost went to sleep, lagged behind, stumbled and fell. The moment a song was struck up the men stepped out briskly.

Over the years a number of well-known songs and tunes have become inextricably linked with different wars. In this chapter I have identified a selection of those historic songs – and the stories behind them – that helped to inspire both sides. Before doing so, however, it is worth considering the author of the above sentiments in more detail, beginning in song.

'A MODERN MAJOR GENERAL'

I am the very model of a modern Major General,
I've information vegetable, animal, and mineral,
I know the kings of England, and I quote the fights historical
From Marathon to Waterloo, in order categorical;

I'm very well acquainted, too, with matters mathematical,
I understand equations, both the simple and quadratical,
About binomial theorem I'm teeming with a lot o' news,
With many cheerful facts about the square of the hypotenuse.

Chorus: *With many cheerful facts about the square of the*
        hypotenuse.

I'm very good at integral and differential calculus;
I know the scientific names of beings animalculous:
In short, in matters vegetable, animal, and mineral,
I am the very model of a modern Major General.

Chorus: *In short, in matters vegetable, animal, and mineral,*
        I am the very model of a modern Major General.

I know our mythic history, King Arthur's and Sir Caradoc's;
I answer hard acrostics, I've a pretty taste for paradox,
I quote in elegiacs all the crimes of Heliogabalus,
In conics I can floor peculiarities parabolous;

I can tell undoubted Raphaels from Gerard Dows and Zoffanies,
I know the croaking chorus from The Frogs of Aristophanes!
Then I can hum a fugue of which I've heard the music's din afore,
And whistle all the airs from that infernal nonsense Pinafore.

Chorus: *And whistle all the airs from that infernal nonsense*
      Pinafore.

Then I can write a washing bill in Babylonic cuneiform,
And tell you ev'ry detail of Caractacus's uniform:
In short, in matters vegetable, animal, and mineral,
I am the very model of a modern Major General.

Chorus: *In short, in matters vegetable, animal, and mineral,*
      I am the very model of a modern Major General.

In fact, when I know what is meant by 'mamelon' and 'ravelin',
When I can tell at sight a Mauser rifle from a Javelin,
When such affairs as sorties and surprises I'm more wary at,
And when I know precisely what is meant by 'commissariat',

When I have learnt what progress has been made in
      modern gunnery,
When I know more of tactics than a novice in a nunnery –
In short, when I've a smattering of elemental strategy –
You'll say a better Major General has never sat a gee.

Chorus: *You'll say a better Major General has never sat a gee.*

For my military knowledge, though I'm plucky and adventury,
Has only been brought down to the beginning of the century;
But still, in matters vegetable, animal, and mineral,
I am the very model of a modern Major General.

Chorus: *But still, in matters vegetable, animal, and mineral,*
      I am the very model of a modern Major General.

Major General Sir Garnet Wolseley, the most distinguished soldier of his day, was the subject of this song in the operetta *The Pirates of Penzance*, with music by Arthur Sullivan and libretto by W. S. Gilbert. For thirty-three years after he was commissioned in 1852, there was scarcely a major campaign involving the British Army in which Garnet Wolseley was not either engaged or in command, from Burma in 1852 to the Sudan in 1885. He even took leave to observe the American Civil War, meeting many of the senior Confederate generals in the process. When in command on operations, he surrounded himself with a small group of carefully selected officers, known as the 'Wolseley Ring'. Such was his reputation for organisation and efficiency that, when all was going well, it was a case of 'Everything's all Sir Garnet', in the fashionable saying of the day.

The Pirates of Penzance had its official première at Fifth Avenue Theater, New York on 31 December 1879, by which time Wolseley was High Commissioner in Southern Africa, in the rank of brevet general. According to Ian Bradley, in *The Annotated Gilbert and Sullivan* (Harmondsworth, Penguin, 1984), Sir Garnet Wolseley, far from taking offence, sometimes sang 'I am the very model of a modern Major General' to entertain family and friends. His tragedy was that, when he finally succeeded the Duke of Cambridge, who was then seventy-six years old and had been Commander-in-Chief of the British Army for thirty-nine years, Wolseley was already sixty-three years old and his best years were behind him. In any event a new Order in Council limited his tenure to just five years.

As Colonel Garnet Wolseley, he was the author of *The Soldier's Pocket-Book for Field Service*, first published in 1869, when he was just thirty-six years old. Reading it today reminds one what an extraordinarily forceful and far-thinking character he must have been, while, at the same time, sympathising with much of the sentiment behind Gilbert's libretto. For example, Wolseley writes on page 13 that: 'It is taken for granted that every officer has a fair knowledge of arithmetic, of at least the first two books of Euclid, of plane geometry, of algebra, as far as quadratic equations, and of permanent fortification. They should also be able at a glance to distinguish the common vegetable productions, including the various species of timber.' In fact, one senses that Gilbert simply must have had *The Soldier's Pocket-Book for Field Service* to hand when he was writing his jaunty and slightly mocking song.

The author sets the tone in the first paragraph, with very wise – and still highly relevant – words on 'Advice to Officers on Service, as regards their bearing towards their Men':

> The relation existing between the rank and file and officers of our army, although peculiar, is not a subject upon which much reflection is common. To officers brought up in regiments, accustomed to see the ordinary routine of military life go on as a machine, it seldom occurs that any change could be made for the better. In fact, many pass their lives without discovering that the military career has any higher aim, than that of moving men on parade by a most complicated process called drill, and that of keeping order amongst them at all times by a rigid system of espionage, which is believed to be discipline. There is but little real sympathy between them and their men. Forgetting that the feudal system has passed away, as long as they do their duty by their soldiers, they expect to find them always ready to obey their nod, and to stand by them in all moments of peril. Pages may easily be filled in narrating the gallant deeds of our officers, and in recounting instances of their reckless personal exposure to save the lives of those under their command.

Creditable as such conduct is, more still is expected of them. They must make themselves loved as well as respected. In our intercourse with the rank and file, we must make them realise that all our interests are identical, causing the latest-joined recruit to feel, that success is of as much real moment to him as it can be to the general. Let us sink as far as possible the respective titles of officers, sergeants, and privates, merging them into the one great professional cognomen of soldier, causing all ranks to feel that it is a noble title of which the general as well as the private may well be proud. Let us give up the phrase 'officer and gentleman,' substituting that of 'soldier' for it; let the word officer be used as seldom as possible, so that the private may really feel that there is no gulf between him and his commander, but that they are merely separated by a ladder, the rungs of which all can equally aspire to mount.

The question of love and respect is a most interesting one. General William Westmoreland, who directed military operations in Vietnam from 1964 to 1968, before serving as US Chief of Staff from 1968 to 1972, once said: 'I don't think I have been loved by my troops, but I think I have been respected.' In writing about her brother, who was killed in Italy while serving with the 11th Battalion, The Sherwood Foresters, Vera Brittain remembered: 'I had heard, from time to time, a good deal from Edward about his youthful C.O., for whom he seemed to have great respect without much affection.' Edward Brittain's Commanding Officer was the gallant Lieutenant Colonel Charles Hudson VC DSO and bar MC. Norman Dixon wrote that, for a certain type of leadership, which he called 'social specialist': 'Not very surprisingly, the most important attribute of such a leader is that he should be liked. Efficiency and task-ability are of rather secondary importance.' My own opinion is that, while respect of one's leader – or, more colloquially, boss – is absolutely essential, 'love' or 'like' are much less important. Of course, in an ideal world, there would be ticks in both boxes.

Apropos Wolseley's final point, about rungs, only one man has risen, through all the ranks in his part of the Service, to the top of the British Army. Having been educated in the local church school, William Robert 'Wully' Robertson went into 'service' in the household of the Earl of Cardigan. In November 1877, though under-age, he enlisted for twelve years' service with the 16th (The Queen's) Lancers. Eight years later, he was promoted to Troop Sergeant-Major, before being commissioned into the 3rd Dragoon Guards on 27 June 1888. When Robertson attended the Staff College at Camberley, nominated by General Sir George White, Commander-in-Chief, India, he was the first former 'ranker' to do so and passed out second in December 1898. Appointed Chief of the Imperial General Staff, the professional Head of the British Army, on 23 December 1915, he served in that position for almost half the First World War, until forced to resign on 28 February 1918. At the end of the war, he was thanked by Parliament, awarded £10,000 and created a baronet, of Beaconsfield in Buckinghamshire. Very appropriately, his autobiography was called *From Private to Field Marshal* (1921). Although 'Wully' Robertson never served under Sir Garnet Wolseley directly, the latter would surely have approved wholeheartedly of an astonishing and meteoric career.

Sir Garnet Wolseley offered some distinctly risky – indeed almost foolhardy – advice:

> *In action*, to be cool and to seem ignorant that any danger exists, is of the first consequence; you must at the same time, however, evince a lively interest in all that is going on: come what may, have a smiling face. If your men are under a fire to which they are not replying, walk about in front of them as they are lying down. I do not mean that you are never to avail yourself of cover, for when skirmishing it is your duty to do so, but under the above-mentioned circumstances the best troops are prone to become unsteady, and it is then the especial duty of officers to set an example of coolness and steadiness. When wounded, officers should take a pride in refusing the assistance of their men to take them to the rear; men are only too fond of helping their wounded comrades out of fire, and when once away, it is difficult to get them back again. All must learn to wait for the ambulance.

While this is all very well in the classroom, it can be a recipe for disaster when in contact with a determined foe. At the Battle of Spion Kop officer casualties far outnumbered, proportionally, those of the men, with the result that there were soon very few leaders left on the mountain itself, while there were no ambulances for miles around.

Wolseley also had some interesting observations on the subject of 'Field Equipment for Officers': 'Englishmen are so fond of their tub, and so particular as to the cleanliness of their persons, that many think it impossible to forego such luxuries; but it is surprising how soon one can learn to do without them. We are too prone to overload ourselves with baggage in the field; it is a saying abroad that 'chaque officier anglais a sa basinoire'.

This 'chaff' comes home to us with only too much truth.' The
French Army had another way of dealing with such eccentrici-
ties, as Lieutenant Henry Clifford remembered in the Crimea:
'When in February 1855 Lord Rokeby arrived to take over the
Guards Brigade from General H. J. Bentinck he brought with
him a patent water closet which was promptly stolen by those
engaging thieves, the Zouaves, in order to make soup in.' British
officers were not alone in feeling that any fool could be uncomfortable. When the Italians were routed in North Africa in early
1941, Desmond Young recorded that the spoils of war included
'clean sheets, and comfortable beds, silk shirts, elaborate toi-
let seats in Florentine leather, scent and scented 'hair muck',
becoming blue cavalry cloaks, *vino* and *liquore* of all varieties,
Pellegrino water in profusion, to say nothing of a motor-caravan
of young women, 'officers for the use of' … The Italians went
to war in comfort.'

W. S. Gilbert rightly observed that Wolseley had 'information
vegetable, animal, and mineral', with the latter advising that
'young nettles, sweet docks, turnip tops, or the young leaves of
mangel-wurzel make good green food. A little salt and pepper
should be added to season them. Dandelion leaves, especially
when young, make a most agreeable salad.' On the subject of
horses, Wolseley wrote: '*Shoeing* – It is much to be regretted that
all officers in passing out of the Staff College, should not be
obliged to learn how to shoe a horse. I strongly advise all who
have an opportunity of learning, to avail themselves of it. A set
of spare shoes, with nails, should be carried on service with
every horse: these shoes should be especially made to fit each
horse; and when a shoe is cast, not a moment should be lost

in having it replaced.' The logic is impeccable and irrefutable: in just the same way that Sir Bradley Wiggins is surely able to fix a puncture.

The detail is quite astonishing and the only surprise is that it absorbed Sir Garnet's leisure hours for a mere four years:

Camels are used in the East from 8 to 16 years; about 7 ft. high (to top of hump), about 8 ft. long from nose to tail. Pace about 2 miles an hour, kept up steadily for the longest marches; load for work on service about 400 to 450 lbs. They thrive well upon leaves of trees, and can go without water longer than any other animal. During temporary halts the laden camel can kneel down and rest. They are admirably adapted for carrying long articles, such as scaling ladders, infantry pontoons, &c. The camel is at home in the desert, and works well in the plains of India; it is unsuited to hilly countries. After rain in clay soil, and over rocks and stony places, they split up and are consequently useless there. They are good for fording rivers that are deep but not rapid, and where (as is so common in India) the bottom of the ford is shifting sand, the passage of a number of camels over it renders it hard and firm. The camel used in India is a vicious brute. Average weight about 1,170 lbs.

Between 1860 and 1907 some 10,000 camels were shipped to Australia from India and Palestine: with more than 400,000 feral camels now living in the outback, aerial culls have begun.

For the metalling of roads, Wolseley's knowledge of minerals proved invaluable: 'The best stone is that which is hardest to break up, such as whinstones, basalts, granites, and beach pebbles; soft granites, sandstones, and the ordinary limestones are bad, but for military roads whatever may be the stone at hand it must be used; if there are several kinds available, but in limited quantities, the hardest description should be reserved for the surface.' The author certainly knew his vegetables, animals and minerals.

In many respects, Sir Garnet was ahead of his time, anticipating how new technology would change the nature of warfare: 'In all wars of this and future ages, the electric telegraph will be greatly used ... In all future wars, the main lines of supply will, in civilized countries, be along railroads. Indeed, when the contest is likely to be a protracted one, and the topography of the country is favourable, it will often be advisable to lay down a railway temporarily, as we did in the Crimea and Abyssinia. We were the first nation that demonstrated how feasible and useful it was to do so.' However prescient he might have been, Wolseley, who had died the year before, never predicted the influence of the railway on the outbreak of war, as outlined by A. J. P. Taylor in his 1969 book, published by Macdonald, *War by Timetable: How the First World War Began*.

Another example of his anticipation of change came in 1862, when the then-Major Garnet Wolseley took leave from his military duties in Canada in order to 'observe' the American Civil War. Having crossing the Potomac River in a blockade runner, he met with a number of Confederate generals, including Robert E. Lee, James Longstreet and Stonewall Jackson. At the same time, Graf Ferdinand von Zeppelin was a civilian observer with the Union Army and Wolseley soon learned that they were making use of balloons for both observation and artillery fire direction. Although Wolseley failed – rather unusually – to anticipate that man would soon take to the air in an unfettered manner, he wrote:

One of the most effective means of learning the whereabouts and doings of an enemy is by means of balloons, for although the undulations of the ground when viewed from the car of a balloon at an elevation of 1,000 or 1,200 feet do not show, yet the position of troops can be accurately ascertained in close, still weather.

Ascents by night, particularly in wooded countries, are most useful for this purpose, as the fires indicate the enemy's position, and his number may be roughly estimated, by allowing ten men to each fire. During an action, a staff officer in a balloon at such an elevation would be of infinite service. The ascent should be made from some height about a mile in rear of the skirmishers;

a telegraphic wire from the car should lead to the spot where
the general in command had established himself, who could
then be kept acquainted with where the enemy's reserves were
posted, etc.

Little more than a year after publication, the French made
considerable use of balloons during the Siege of Paris: 66
balloons were launched, bearing 102 passengers, 11 tons of
mail and some 400 carrier pigeons to carry the self-addressed
envelopes (SAE) back across the Prussian siege lines. Despite
Sir Garnet's foresight, the British Army neglected to open
a School of Ballooning, at Chatham in Kent, until 1888,
because the investment was deemed too costly. Some things
never change.

'OVER THE HILLS AND FAR AWAY'

The traditional English song, 'Over the Hills and Far Away',
given a military feel by George Farquhar in his comedy,
The Recruiting Officer (1706), was based on the play-
wright's experiences as an officer in the Earl of Orrery's
Regiment of Foot:

> *Our 'prentice Tom may now refuse*
> *To wipe his scoundrel Master's Shoes,*
> *For now he's free to sing and play*
> *Over the Hills and far away.*
> *Over the Hills and O'er the Main,*
> *To Flanders, Portugal and Spain,*
> *The Queen commands and we'll obey*
> *Over the Hills and far away.*

We all shall lead more happy lives
  By getting rid of brats and wives
That scold and bawl both night and day –
  Over the Hills and far away.
Over the Hills and O'er the Main,
  To Flanders, Portugal and Spain,
The Queen commands and we'll obey
  Over the Hills and far away.

Courage, boys, 'tis one to ten,
  But we return all gentlemen
All gentlemen as well as they,
  Over the Hills and far away.
Over the Hills and O'er the Main,
  To Flanders, Portugal and Spain,
The Queen commands and we'll obey
  Over the Hills and far away.

While the tune has remained the same, the lyrics have changed frequently over the years and were recently rewritten for each new *Sharpe* TV film, about the experiences of Richard Sharpe with the 95th Regiment, based on a series of novels by Bernard Cornwell. 'Over the Hills and Far Away' is a favourite of The Rifles: although the regiment was formed only on 1 February 2007, it counts amongst its antecedents no fewer than twenty-two of the 109 regiments of foot in Queen Victoria's army.

'THE BRITISH GRENADIERS'

The tune of 'The British Grenadiers', introduced to Britain during the reign of King William III, is the Regimental Quick

March of the Royal Regiment of Artillery, the Corps of Royal Engineers, the Honourable Artillery Company, the Grenadier Guards and the Royal Regiment of Fusiliers. While the tune first became associated with the Grenadier Guards in 1706, the lyrics date from around 1750:

Some talk of Alexander, and some of Hercules
  Of Hector and Lysander, and such great names as these.
But of all the world's great heroes, there's none that can compare.
  With a tow, row, row, row, row, row, to the British Grenadiers.

Those heroes of antiquity ne'er saw a cannon ball,
  Or knew the force of powder to slay their foes withal.
But our brave boys do know it, and banish all their fears,
  Sing tow, row, row, row, row, row, for the British Grenadiers.

Whene'er we are commanded to storm the palisades,
  Our leaders march with fusees, and we with hand grenades.
We throw them from the glacis, about the enemies' ears.
  Sing tow, row, row, row, row, row, the British Grenadiers.

And when the siege is over, we to the town repair.
  The townsmen cry, 'Hurrah, boys, here comes a Grenadier!
Here come the Grenadiers, my boys, who know no doubts or fears!'
  Then sing tow, row, row, row, row, row, the British Grenadiers.

Then let us fill a bumper, and drink a health to those
  Who carry caps and pouches, and wear the loupèd clothes.
May they and their commanders live happy all their years.
  With a tow, row, row, row, row, row, for the British Grenadiers.'

Poignantly, during Operation Market Garden, the combined ground and airborne assault on Arnhem, in mid-September

1944, men of 1st (British) Airborne Division played *The British Grenadiers* on whatever instruments they had to hand, including a flute, with tin helmets standing in for drums.

'HOT STUFF'

This version of the song, 'Hot Stuff', has nothing whatever to do with Donna Summer. Sung to the tune 'Lilies of France', it was written by Ned Botwood, Sergeant of Grenadiers of the 47th Regiment of Foot, and made its first appearance in Rivington's *New York Gazetteer* on 5 May 1774:

> *Come, each death-doing dog that dares venture his neck,*
> *Come, follow the hero that goes to Quebec;*
> *Jump aboard of the transports, and loose every sail,*
> *Pay your debts at the tavern by giving leg-bail;*
> *And ye that love fighting shall soon have enough;*
> *Wolfe commands us, my boys, we shall give them Hot Stuff.*
>
> *Up the River St. Lawrence our troops shall advance,*
> *To the Grenadier's March we will teach them to dance.*
> *Cape Breton we've taken and next we will try*
> *At the capital to give them another black eye.*
> *Vaudreuil, 'tis in vain you pretend to look gruff,*
> *Those are coming who know how to give you Hot Stuff.*
>
> *With powder in his periwig, and snuff in his nose,*
> *Monsieur will run down our descent to oppose;*
> *And the Indians will come, but the Light Infantry*
> *Will soon compel them to betake to a tree.*
> *From such rascals as these may we fear a rebuff?*
> *Advance, grenadiers, and let fly your Hot Stuff!*

When the Forty-seventh Regiment is dashing ashore,
*   When bullets are whistling and cannon do roar,*
Says Montcalm, 'Those are Shirley's, I know their lapels.'
*   'You lie,' says Ned Botwood, 'We are of Lascelles!*
Though our clothing is changed, yet we scorn a powder-puff;
*   So at you, ye bitches, here's give you Hot Stuff.'*

With Monkton and Townsend, those brave brigadiers,
*   I think we shall soon have the town 'bout their ears,*
And when we have done with the mortars and guns,
*   If you please, Madam Abbess, a word with your nuns.*
Each soldier shall enter the convent in buff
*   And then, never fear, we will give them Hot Stuff.*

On 31 July 1759, Sergeant Ned Botwood was killed at the Battle of Montmorency – also known as the Battle of Beauport – when a British force, under the command of General James Wolfe, was thrown back from the French defensive line at Beauport, some three miles east of Quebec.

'THE WORLD TURNED UPSIDE DOWN'

George Thomason, a contemporary bookseller, put together a compilation of Civil War pamphlets and newsletters, known as the Thomason Tracts, amongst which is the 1646 ballad, 'The World Turned Upside Down':

Listen to me and you shall hear, news hath not been this
*   thousand year:*
Since Herod, Caesar, *and many more, you never heard the*
*   like before,*
Holy-dayes are despis'd, new fashions are devis'd,

Old Christmas is kickt out of Town.
Yet let's be content, and the times lament, you see the world
turn'd upside down.

The wise men did rejoyce to see our Savior Christs Nativity:
The Angels did good tidings bring, the Sheepheards did rejoyce
and sing,
Let all honest men, take example by them,
Why should we from good Laws be bound?
Yet let's be content, &c.

Command is given, we must obey, and quite forget old
Christmas day:
Kill a thousand men, or a Town regain, we will give thanks and
praise amain,
The wine pot shall clinke, we will feast and drinke,
And then strange motions will abound.
Yet let's be content, &c.

Our Lords and Knights, and Gentry too, doe mean old fashions
to forgoe:
They set a porter at the gate, that none must enter in thereat,
They count it a sin, when poor people come in,
Hospitality it selfe is drown'd.
Yet let's be content, &c.

The serving men doe sit and whine, and thinke it long ere
dinner time:
The Butler's still out of the way, or else my Lady keeps the key,
The poor old cook, in the larder doth look,
Where is no goodnesse to be found,
Yet let's be content, &c.

*To conclude, I'le tell you news that's right, Christmas was kil'd
    at Naseby fight:*
*Charity was slain at that same time, Jack Tell troth too, a
    friend of mine,*
Likewise then did die, rost beef and shred pie,
Pig, Goose and Capon no quarter found.
*Yet let's be content, and the times lament, you see the world
    turn'd upside down.*

In the light of the traumatic and unexpected experiences that they had undergone during six years of war, 'The World Turned Upside Down' seems an entirely appropriate tune for the British band to have played as General O'Hara surrendered, on behalf of General Lord Cornwallis, to George Washington and the Comte de Rochambeau at Yorktown on 19 October 1781.

'THE BATTLE HYMN OF THE REPUBLIC'

After listening to the singing of the men of the 6th Wisconsin Volunteer Infantry during a review at Upton Hill, Virginia, on 18 November 1861, Julia Ward Howe spent the night at the Willard Hotel in Washington. With the rousing tune still ringing in her ears, she described her experiences: 'I went to bed that night as usual, and slept, according to my wont, quite soundly. I awoke in the gray of the morning twilight; and as I lay waiting for the dawn, the long lines of the desired poem began to twine themselves in my mind. Having thought out all the stanzas, I said to myself, "I must get up and write these verses down, lest I fall asleep again and forget them." So, with a sudden effort, I sprang out of bed, and found in the dimness an old stump of a pen which I remembered to have used the day before. I scrawled the verses almost without looking at the paper.'

While the words of 'The Battle Hymn of the Republic' were first published in *The Atlantic Monthly* in February 1862, it was a fortuitous melding of words and tune that guaranteed its lasting popularity. Some six years earlier, William Steffe had written a tune which soon spread across the country as a campfire spiritual. Inspired by the events at Harper's Ferry in October 1859 – as well as the fact one of their number was a soldier by the name of John Brown – the men of the 2nd Infantry Battalion, Massachusetts Militia collectively wrote the words 'John Brown's Body', which they then sang to Steffe's tune. 'The Battle Hymn of the Republic' was adopted by the Unionist cause and swiftly became popular with the soldiery. Often heard at both the Republican Party and Democratic Party conventions, it was also sung at the funeral of Sir Winston Churchill and at the official memorial services in Washington and London following the attacks of 11 September 2001.

Mine eyes have seen the glory of the coming of the Lord:
He is trampling out the vintage where the grapes of wrath
are stored;
He hath loosed the fateful lightning of His terrible swift sword:
His truth is marching on.

Chorus:
Glory, glory, hallelujah!
Glory, glory, hallelujah!
Glory, glory, hallelujah!
His truth is marching on.

I have seen Him in the watch-fires of a hundred circling camps,
They have builded Him an altar in the evening dews and damps;

I can read His righteous sentence by the dim and flaring lamps:
  His day is marching on.

[Chorus]

I have read a fiery gospel writ in burnished rows of steel:
  'As ye deal with my contemners, so with you my grace
      shall deal;
Let the Hero, born of woman, crush the serpent with his heel,
  His truth is marching on.'

[Chorus]

He has sounded forth the trumpet that shall never call retreat;
  He is sifting out the hearts of men before His judgment-seat:
Oh, be swift, my soul, to answer Him! be jubilant, my feet!
  Our God is marching on.

[Chorus]

In the beauty of the lilies Christ was born across the sea,
  With a glory in His bosom that transfigures you and me:
As He died to make men holy, let us die to make men free,
  While God is marching on.

[Chorus]

He is coming like the glory of the morning on the wave,
  He is Wisdom to the mighty, He is Succor to the brave,
So the world shall be His footstool, and the soul of Time His slave,
  Our God is marching on.

[Chorus]

'GOODBYE DOLLY GRAY'

A music hall song, written by Will D. Cobb and set to music by Paul Barnes, 'Goodbye Dolly Gray' was sung by American soldiers during the Spanish-American War of 1898, which led to Cuban independence and the loss of Spanish suzerainty over the Philippines, Puerto Rico and Guam. The song later became enormously popular during the Second Anglo-Boer War.

> *I have come to say goodbye, Dolly Gray,*
> *It's no use to ask me why, Dolly Gray,*
> *There's a murmur in the air, you can hear it everywhere,*
> *It's the time to do and dare, Dolly Gray.*

> *So if you hear the sound of feet, Dolly Gray,*
> *Sounding through the village street, Dolly Gray,*
> *It's the tramp of soldiers' true in their uniforms so blue,*
> *I must say goodbye to you, Dolly Gray.*

> *Goodbye Dolly I must leave you, though it breaks my heart to go,*
> *Something tells me I am needed at the front to fight the foe,*
> *See – the boys in blue are marching and I can no longer stay,*
> *Hark – I hear the bugle calling, goodbye Dolly Gray.*

'IT'S A LONG WAY TO TIPPERARY'

Legend has it that the music for 'It's a Long Way to Tipperary' was co-written by Jack Judge and Harry J. Williams for a five-shilling bet at Stalybridge, Greater Manchester, on 30 January 1912, before being performed the following night in the town's Grand Theatre. What is certainly true is that both Judge's parents were Irish, with strong Tipperary connections, while the first line of the refrain was engraved on Williams's tombstone at Temple Balsall, Warwickshire. The following year, 'It's a Long Way to Tipperary' was first sung on the stage by Florrie Forde, an Australian singer who became one of the stars of early twentieth-century music hall. On 13 August 1914, the Connaught Rangers sang 'It's a Long Way to Tipperary' as they marched through Boulogne, as reported by George Curnock in the *Daily Mail* on 18 August 1914:

Up to mighty London
  Came an Irishman one day.
As the streets are paved with gold
  Sure, everyone was gay,
Singing songs of Piccadilly,
  Strand and Leicester Square,
Till Paddy got excited,
  Then he shouted to them there:

Chorus:
It's a long way to Tipperary,
  It's a long way to go.
It's a long way to Tipperary
  To the sweetest girl I know!
Goodbye, Piccadilly,
  Farewell, Leicester Square!
It's a long long way to Tipperary,
  But my heart's right there.

Paddy wrote a letter
  To his Irish Molly-O,
Saying, 'Should you not receive it,
  Write and let me know!'
'If I make mistakes in spelling,
  Molly, dear,' said he,

'Remember, it's the pen that's bad,
Don't lay the blame on me!'

[Chorus]

Molly wrote a neat reply
To Irish Paddy-O,
Saying 'Mike Maloney
Wants to marry me, and so
Leave the Strand and Piccadilly
Or you'll be to blame,
For love has fairly drove me silly:
Hoping you're the same!'

[Chorus]

'PACK UP YOUR TROUBLES IN YOUR OLD KIT-BAG'

Written by George Henry Powell, using his pseudonym, George Asaf, and set to music by his brother, Felix Powell, 'Pack up Your Troubles in Your Old Kit-bag' was first published in 1915:

Pack up your troubles in your old kit-bag,
  And smile, smile, smile.
While you've a Lucifer to light your fag,
  Smile, boys, that's the style.
What's the use of worrying?
  It never was worth while, so
Pack up your troubles in your old kit-bag,
  And smile, smile, smile.

The next two, hugely popular, First World War songs would no doubt have greatly upset Lord Kitchener, in the light of his strictures about women and wine; however, he probably knew nothing about them, having drowned on 5 June 1916 when HMS *Hampshire*, in which he was sailing from Scapa Flow to northern Russia for talks, sank after striking a German submarine-laid mine off Orkney.

'MADEMOISELLE FROM ARMENTIÈRES'

While the tune is an old one, dating back to the 1830s, there are a number of claimants for this song, although nothing has been conclusively proved. It has spawned a range of different lyrics – some of which are rather risqué – as well as a film of the same name and a number of television appearances. While 'It's a Long Way to Tipperary' is the second part, 'Mademoiselle from Armentières' is the third part of the regimental march of Princess Patricia's Canadian Light Infantry, usually referred to as the PPCLI.

> *O Madam, have you any good wine?*
>   *Parlez-vous;*
> *O Madam, have you any good wine?*
>   *Parlez-vous;*
> *O Madam, have you any good wine?*
>   *Fit for a soldier of the line?*
> *Hinky-dinky, parlez-vous.*

'GOODBYE-EE!'

Written and composed in 1917 by R. P. Weston and Bert Lee, 'Goodbye-ee!' was sung by Florrie Forde, Daisy Wood and Chas Whittle.

> *Goodbye-ee! goodbye-ee!*
>   *Wipe the tear, baby dear, from your eye-ee.*
> *Tho' it's hard to part, I know,*
>   *I'll be tickled to death to go.*
> *Don't cry-ee! – don't sigh-ee! –*
>   *There's a silver lining in the sky-ee! –*
> *Bonsoir, old thing! cheerio! chin-chin!*
>   *Nahpoo! Toodle-oo! Goodbye-ee!*

The word 'nahpoo' is soldiers' slang from the First World War, derived from the French, 'il n'y en a plus' or, in translation, 'there is no more of it'. In *1066 And All That*, Sellar and

Yeatman refer, in the context of eighteenth-century Indian 'potentates', to 'the terrible Napoo Sahib'.

'THE WHITE CLIFFS OF DOVER'

With words by Nat Burton – an American who had never been to England, let alone to Dover – and music by Walter Kent, 'The White Cliffs of Dover' was first published in 1941. Having become a huge hit in the United States the following year, it was popularised this side of the Atlantic by Vera Lynn, who first recorded the song the same year:

There'll be bluebirds over
   The white cliffs of Dover
Tomorrow
   Just you wait and see.

I'll never forget the people I met
   Braving those angry skies
I remember well as the shadows fell
   The light of hope in their eyes.

And though I'm far away
   I still can hear them say
Bombs up …
   But when the dawn comes up.

There'll be bluebirds over
   The white cliffs of Dover
Tomorrow
   Just you wait and see.

There'll be love and laughter
  And peace ever after
Tomorrow
  When the world is free.

The shepherd will tend his sheep
  The valley will bloom again
And Jimmy will go to sleep
  In his own little room again.

There'll be bluebirds over
  The white cliffs of Dover
Tomorrow
  Just you wait and see.

'LILI MARLEEN'

Written in 1915 by Hans Leip, a schoolmaster from Hamburg conscripted into the German Army, 'Lili Marleen', also known as 'Lili Marlene', was first published, with two extra verses, as 'Das Lied eines jungen Soldaten auf der Wacht', or 'The Song of a Young Soldier on Watch', in 1937. Set to music the following year by Norbert Schultze, 'Lili Marleen' was recorded by Lale Andersen in 1939 and, most unusually, became a favourite with both Axis and Allied forces after being played on Soldatensender Belgrad (Soldiers' Radio Belgrade) in 1941. In his memoirs, Field Marshal Earl Alexander of Tunis described the song as 'curiously seductive and nostalgic', noting that it 'lulled both armies to sleep'. Tommie Connor's lyrics, written in 1944, were recorded by Perry Como on 27 June that year and also by Vera Lynn:

Vor der Kaserne,
  Vor dem großen Tor,
Stand eine Laterne,
  Und steht sie noch davor,
So woll'n wir uns da wieder seh'n,
  Bei der Laterne wollen wir steh'n,
Wie einst, Lili Marleen.

Unsere beiden Schatten,
  Sah'n wie einer aus,
Daß wir so lieb uns hatten,
  Das sah man gleich daraus.
Und alle Leute soll'n es seh'n,
  Wenn wir bei der
    Laterne steh'n,
Wie einst, Lili Marleen.

Schon rief der Posten:
  Sie blasen Zapfenstreich,
Es kann drei Tage kosten!
  Kamerad, ich komm' ja gleich.
Da sagten wir Aufwiederseh'n.
  Wie gerne wollt' ich mit
    dir geh'n,
Mit dir, Lili Marleen!

Deine Schritte kennt sie,
  Deinen zieren Gang.
Alle Abend brennt sie,
  Doch mich vergaß sie lang.
Und sollte mir ein Leid gescheh'n,
  Wer wird bei der Laterne steh'n,
Mit dir, Lili Marleen!

Underneath the lantern
  By the barrack gate,
Darling I remember
  The way you used to wait.
T'was there that you
    whispered tenderly
  That you loved me;
You'd always be
  My Lili of the lamplight,
My own Lili Marleen.

Time would come for roll call,
  Time for us to part,
Darling I'd caress you
  And press you to my heart,
And there 'neath that far-off
    lantern light,
  I'd hold you tight,
We'd kiss good night,
  My Lili of the lamplight,
My own Lili Marleen.

Orders came for sailing,
  Somewhere over there.
All confined to barracks
  Was more than I could
    bear.
I knew you were waiting in
    the street,
  I heard your feet
But could not meet
  My Lili of the lamplight
My own Lili Marleen.

Aus dem stillen Raume,
  Aus der Erde Grund,
Hebt mich wie im Traume
  Dein verliebter Mund.
Wenn sich die späten
  Nebel dreh'n,
  Werd' ich bei der Laterne
    steh'n
Wie einst, Lili Marleen!

Resting in our billets
  Just behind the lines,
Even tho' we're parted,
  Your lips are close to mine.
You wait where that lantern
    softly gleams,
  Your sweet face seems
To haunt my dreams,
    My Lili of the lamplight,
  My own Lili Marleen.

'LOVE FAREWELL'

The eighteenth-century melody, 'Love Farewell', with lyrics by the folk musician, John Tams, was also used in the *Sharpe* TV films. In December 2009, Tams recorded a version of 'Love Farewell' with the Band and Bugles of The Rifles, in order to raise money for the military charity, Help for Heroes:

I thought I heard the Colonel crying:
  'March brave boys', there's no denying
Cannons roaring – drums a-beating
  'March brave boys, there's no retreating,'
Love Farewell.

If I should fall in far off battle
  Cannons roar and rifles rattle;
Thoughts fly homeward – words unspoken
  Valiant hearts are oft times broken,
Love Farewell.

Will you go or will you tarry?
    Will you wait or will you marry?
Would this moment last for ever
    Kiss me now and leave me never,
Love Farewell.

I thought I heard the Colonel crying:
    'March brave boys', there's no denying
Cannons roaring – drums a-beating
    'March brave boys, there's no retreating,'
Love Farewell.

Oh Judy should I die in glory
    In The Times *you'll read my story;*
But I'm so bothered by your charms
    I'd rather die within your arms,
Love Farewell.

Prayers

In a war between Christian nations, both sides felt that God was on their side. During the First World War, German soldiers had 'Gott mit uns' – 'God with us' – on either their helmets or, later, on their belt buckles, a tradition that continued during the Second World War. Religion naturally assumed greater prominence during times of conflict, culminating in the writing of a number of very moving prayers:

THE PRAYERS OF SIR FRANCIS DRAKE

Sir Francis Drake wrote two well-known prayers. The longer one was written in his ship's diary in 1577, before he embarked on a hazardous and uncertain voyage of discovery and pillage to South America:

Disturb us, Lord, when we are too pleased with ourselves; when our dreams have come true because we dreamed too little; when we arrived safely because we sailed too close to the shore.

Disturb us, Lord, when with the abundance of things we possess we have lost our thirst for the waters of life; having fallen in love with life, we have ceased to dream of eternity and in our efforts to build a new earth, we have allowed our vision of the new Heaven to dim.

Disturb us, Lord, to dare more boldly, to venture on wilder seas, where storms will show your mastery; where losing sight of land, we shall find the stars.

We ask you to push back the horizons of our hopes; and to push back the future in strength, courage, hope, and love. This we ask in the name of our Captain, who is Jesus Christ.

While at anchor in his ship, the *Elizabeth Bonaventure*, off Cape Sakar on 17 May 1587, after the 'singeing of the King of Spain's beard' at Cadiz and the sacking of Sagres on the Portuguese coast, Sir Francis Drake wrote to Queen Elizabeth I's Secretary of State, Sir Francis Walsingham: 'There must be a begynnyng of any great matter, but the contenewing unto the end untyll it be thoroughly ffynyshed yieldes the trew glory.' These words were adapted by the Very Reverend Eric Milner-White, Dean of York – who had earlier introduced the popular Service of Nine Lessons and Carols at King's College, Cambridge – for the National Day of Prayer on Sunday,

23 March 1941, into the short and simple prayer that is frequently used today:

> *O Lord God, when Thou givest to thy servants to endeavour any*
> *great matter, grant us also to know that it is not the beginning,*
> *but the continuing of the same, until it be thoroughly finished,*
> *which yieldeth the true glory; through Him who, for the finishing*
> *of Thy work, laid down His life for us, our Redeemer, Jesus Christ.*

Shortly before the Battle of El Alamein, Lieutenant General Bernard Montgomery pinned a copy of Drake's prayer up in his battle caravan. It remained there for the rest of the war.

QUEEN ELIZABETH I'S 'A PRAYER, TO BE DELIVERED FROM OUR ENEMIES'

This prayer, a much longer version of which appears in *Annals of the Church under Queen Elizabeth*, was written before the defeat of the Spanish Armada:

> *We do instantly beseech thee of thy gracious goodness, to be mer-*
> *ciful to the Church militant here upon earth, and at this time*
> *compassed about with most strong and subtle adversaries. O, let*
> *thine enemies know that thou hast received England, which they*
> *most of all for thy Gospel's sake do malign, into thine own protec-*
> *tion. Set a wall about it, O Lord, and evermore mightily defend*
> *it. Let it be a comfort to the afflicted, a help to the oppressed,*
> *and a defence to thy Church and people, persecuted abroad. And,*
> *forasmuch as thy cause is now in hand, direct and go before our*
> *armies both by land and sea. Bless them and prosper them, and*
> *grant unto them honourable success and victory. Thou art our*
> *help and shield. Oh, give good and prosperous success to all those*
> *that fight this battle against the enemies of God.*

SIR JACOB ASTLEY'S PRAYER

On Sunday, 23 October 1642, before the Battle of Edgehill, fought between Royalists and Parliamentarians during the English Civil War, Sir Jacob Astley, later 1st Baron Astley of Reading, who had been appointed Major General of the Foot by King Charles I, uttered these words in prayer:

> *O Lord, Thou knowest how busy I must be this day.*
> *If I forget Thee, do not Thou forget me.*

The words surround the base of the memorial to the Chelsea Pensioners, which stands in front of the Chapel, on Royal Hospital Road in Chelsea. Sir Jacob Astley later distinguished himself at the first and second Battles of Newbury and also at the Battle of Naseby, earning himself a mention in 'The Battle of Naseby' by Thomas Babington Macaulay, Lord Macaulay:

> *It was about the noon of a glorious day of June,*
> *That we saw their banners dance and their cuirasses shine,*
> *And the man of blood was there, with his long essenced hair,*
> *And Astley, and Sir Marmaduke, and Rupert of the Rhine.*

THE PRAYER OF VICE ADMIRAL
OF THE WHITE HORATIO NELSON

This prayer was found on the table in Nelson's cabin in HMS *Victory* after the Battle of Trafalgar, fought against the combined fleets of France and Spain on 21 October 1805:

May the great God whom I worship grant to my country, and for the benefit of Europe in general, a great and glorious victory, and may no misconduct in anyone tarnish it; and may humanity after victory be the predominant feature in the British fleet. For myself I commit my life to Him who made me, and may His blessing light upon my endeavours for serving my country faithfully. To Him I resign myself and the just cause which is entrusted to me to defend. Amen. Amen. Amen.

QUEEN VICTORIA'S
NEW YEAR'S PRAYER

On New Year's Eve 1899, during the Second Anglo-Boer War, Queen Victoria wrote in her Journal: 'This is the last day of a very eventful, & in many ways sad year. I have lost many friends, amongst them one who can never be replaced, darling Marie Leiningen. Then there are the sad losses amongst my brave troops, which is a constant sorrow to me. In the midst of it all I have however to thank God for many mercies & for the splendid unity & loyalty of my Empire. – I pray God to bless & preserve all my Children, Grandchildren, & kind relations & friends & may there be brighter days in store for us!'

Sadly, her prayers were not answered. One of her grandsons, Prince Christian Victor of Schleswig-Holstein, who was serving in South Africa with The Rifle Brigade, died of enteric fever at Pretoria on 29 October 1900. The Treaty of Vereeniging, which finally brought the Second Anglo-Boer War to a satisfactory conclusion, was not signed until 31 May 1902, more than sixteen months after the Queen's death.

WILLIAM NOEL HODGSON'S 'BEFORE ACTION'

William Noel Hodgson, son of the first Bishop of St Edmundbury and Ipswich, was educated at Durham School and at Christ Church, Oxford. Known to his fellow officers in The Devonshire Regiment as 'Smiler', he was awarded the Military Cross for his gallantry during the Battle of Loos in the autumn of 1915. As well as prose published under a pseudonym, Edward Melbourne, he wrote poetry. The Reverend Ernest Courtenay Crosse, Chaplain to the 8th and 9th Battalions, The Devonshire Regiment, wrote that there are

> few more beautiful poems during the war than 'Before Action', written by Noel Hodgson, bombing officer of 9th Devons at the time. Hodgson knew quite well that the chances were that he would be killed on the first day of the Battle of the Somme. It wasn't, as sometimes said, a case of premonition. The chances were all in favour of that, and he knew it. Two nights before the attack was due to start he was billeted in a beautiful wood, Le Bois des Tailles, about three miles behind the line. It was lovely summer weather, and even nightingales could be heard at times. In these surroundings Hodgson took up his pen and wrote, with the memory of many wonderful sunsets which he had witnessed from what is perhaps the finest view in all England, Durham Cathedral, as seen from the hill to the west, where the school is situated at which he was educated:

> > *By all the glories of the day*
> > * And the cool evening's benison,*
> > *By that last sunset touch that lay*
> > * Upon the hills when day was done,*
> > *By beauty lavishly outpoured*
> > * And blessings carelessly received,*

By all the days that I have lived
Make me a soldier, Lord.

By all of man's hopes and fears
And all the wonders poets sing,
The laughter of unclouded years,
And every sad and lovely thing:
By the romantic ages stored
With high endeavour that was his,
By all his mad catastrophes
Make me a man, O Lord.

I, that on my familiar hill
Saw with uncomprehending eyes
A hundred of Thy sunsets spill
Their fresh and sanguine sacrifice,
Ere the sun swings his noonday sword
Must say goodbye to all of this:–
By all delights that I shall miss,
Help me to die, O Lord.

Such thoughts as these must have been common to many before a battle. But there are times when a man's thoughts are best left to himself, and though I lived with Hodgson at this time, he never mentioned these to me. I buried him four days later almost on the spot where I found his body, lying beside that of his batman.

Hodgson also wrote 'Take my Youth that Died Today', to which Vera Brittain referred in *Testament of Youth* (London, Victor Gollancz, 1933), her autobiography of the years 1900–25: 'William Noel Hodgson, who when only twenty [sic] was killed on the Somme, similarly lamented this lost youth which we had barely known in one of the saddest little songs that the War produced. It brought me near to weeping, I remember, when after four years of hospitals, and last leaves, and farewells, I heard it sung by Topliss Green at the Albert Hall about 1919.'

R. E. VERNÈDE'S 'A PRAYER TO ENGLAND'

Robert Ernest Vernède was born in London and educated at St Paul's School and at St John's College, Oxford. On the outbreak of the First World War, he was commissioned into The Rifle Brigade. Wounded on the Somme in 1916, he was killed in action on 9 April 1917 while leading an assault on the village of Havrincourt. *War Poems and Other Verses*, in which 'A Prayer to England' was included, was published by William Heinemann (London) later that year:

> *All that a man might ask thou hast given me, England,*
> *Birthright and happy childhood's long hearts-ease,*
> *And love whose range is deep beyond all sounding,*
> *And wider than all seas:*
> *A heart to front the world and find God in it,*
> *Eyes blind enow but not too blind to see*
> *The lovely things behind the dross and darkness,*
> *And lovelier things to be;*
> *And friends whose loyalty time nor death shall weaken,*
> *And quenchless hope and laughter's golden store –*
> *All that a man might ask thou hast given me, England,*
> *Yet grant thou one thing more:*
> *That now when envious foes would spoil thy splendour,*
> *Unversed in arms, a dreamer such as I*
> *May in thy ranks be deemed not all unworthy,*
> *England, for thee to die.*

KING GEORGE VI's
CHRISTMAS BROADCAST 1939

As is now well known, from the 2010 film, *The King's Speech*, King George VI had a real dread of broadcasting on the radio and also of speaking in public. Having avoided doing so for two of the first three years of his reign, he realised that the advent of war required him to make the effort once again. In his diary entry for Christmas Day 1939, he makes his lack of enthusiasm for the task very clear: 'We went to church in the forenoon. Gave the presents to the children, & later to the servants. I broadcast a message to the Empire at the end of the B.B.C. Round the Empire Programme. This is always an ordeal for me, & I don't begin to enjoy Christmas until after it is over.' Nevertheless, having resolved that while the war lasted, he would not wear civilian clothes, King George VI, in the uniform of an Admiral of the Fleet, sat in front of two microphones at Sandringham and addressed the Empire, closing with the following words:

A new year is at hand. We cannot tell what it will bring. If it brings peace, how thankful we shall all be. If it brings continued struggle we shall remain undaunted. In the meantime I feel that we may all find a message of encouragement in the lines which, in my closing words, I would like to say to you:

> *I said to the man*
> *who stood at the gate of the year,*
> *'Give me a light that I may tread safely*
> *into the unknown.'*
>
> *And he replied,*
> *'Go out into the darkness*

and put your hand into the hand of God.
That shall be to you
better than light
and safer than a known way!'

May that Almighty Hand guide and uphold us all.

This address was to have a greater impact than any other Royal Christmas Broadcast. Not only was it perfectly attuned to the moment – the 'Phoney War', or 'Sitzkrieg', as it was ironically known; the prevailing uncertainty; the unfailing resolve; and the sense of an Empire with a common cause – but the BBC was besieged with enquiries about the poem. However,

the King did not know the author's name, having quoted from the last part of a longer poem, sent to him on a Christmas card. The author – who had heard the broadcast but not immediately recognised her own words – was Minnie Louise Haskins, a Sunday school teacher and later a lecturer in Social Sciences at the London School of Economics, who had written the poem in 1908.

One result of the broadcast was the first public publication of a collection of Minnie Louise Haskins's poetry. Another was that J. Arthur Rank used the 'The Gate of the Year' in *The Mortal Storm* (1940). A reworking of an earlier Rank picture called *Turn of the Tide* (1935), the film ends with a family listening to a broadcast in which a recording of the King's Christmas Broadcast was used. Yet a third was that Queen Elizabeth the Queen Mother had the words of the poem engraved on brass plaques, which are affixed to the gates of the King George VI Memorial Chapel at Windsor Castle, where he is buried. The Queen Mother's remains now lie there as well, while the poem was read at her State Funeral on 9 April 2002.

J. G. MAGEE'S 'HIGH FLIGHT'

John Gillespie Magee was born in Shanghai on 9 June 1922, to an American father and a British mother, both of whom were Anglican missionaries. Nine years later, he moved with his mother to England and was educated at Rugby, following in the footsteps of Rupert Brooke, who had been awarded the School Poetry Prize thirty-four years earlier. Although he had been awarded a scholarship, Magee chose not to take his place at Yale, enlisting instead in the Royal Canadian Air Force in October 1940. Soon after earning his wings in Canada in June

1941, he was posted to 412 (Fighter) Squadron, RCAF, based at RAF Digby in Lincolnshire. Flying a Spitfire from RAF Wellingore on 11 December 1941, John Gillespie Magee was involved in a mid-air collision with an Airspeed Oxford – both pilots were killed. Shortly before he died, John Gillespie Magee wrote 'Night Flight':

> *Oh! I have slipped the surly bonds of Earth*
> *   And danced the skies on laughter-silvered wings;*
> *Sunward I've climbed, and joined the tumbling mirth*
> *   of sun-split clouds, – and done a hundred things*
> *You have not dreamed of – wheeled and soared and swung*
> *   High in the sunlit silence. Hov'ring there,*
> *I've chased the shouting wind along, and flung*
> *   My eager craft through footless halls of air …*
>
> *Up, up the long, delirious, burning blue*
> *   I've topped the wind-swept heights with easy grace.*
> *Where never lark, or even eagle flew –*
> *   And, while with silent, lifting mind I've trod*
> *The high untrespassed sanctity of space,*
> *   – Put out my hand, and touched the face of God.*

Unsurprisingly, 'High Flight' has proved extremely popular with airmen and also with astronauts. John Gillespie Magee is buried in Holy Cross Cemetery, Scopwick, Lincolnshire; his gravestone is engraved with the first and last lines of the poem. It is something of a coincidence that perhaps the best-known poem of the First World War, 'In Flanders Fields', which was first published in *Punch* on 8 December 1915, was also written by a Canadian, Lieutenant Colonel John McCrae, MD.

GENERAL DOUGLAS MACARTHUR's 'PRAYER FOR ARTHUR'

Soon after the United States had entered the Second World War, Douglas MacArthur, one of only five officers to have achieved five-star rank in the US Army, wrote this prayer in tribute to his son, Arthur MacArthur IV, who was born in Manila on 21 February 1938:

Build me a son, O Lord, who will be strong enough to know when he is weak, and brave enough to face himself when he is afraid; one who will be proud and unbending in honest defeat, and humble and gentle in victory.

Build me a son whose wishbone will not be where his backbone should be; a son who will know Thee and that to know himself is the foundation stone of knowledge. Lead him, I pray, not in the path of ease and comfort, but under the stress and spur of difficulties and challenge. Here let him learn to stand up in the storm; here let him learn compassion for those who fail.

Build me a son whose heart will be clean, whose goal will be high; a son who will master himself before he seeks to master other men; one who will learn to laugh, yet never forget how to weep; one who will reach into the future, yet never forget the past.

And after all these things are his, add, I pray, enough of a sense of humor, so that he may always be serious, yet never take himself too seriously. Give him humility, so that he may always remember the simplicity of greatness, the open mind of true wisdom, the meekness of true strength.

Then I, his father, will dare to whisper, 'I have not lived in vain.'

Arthur MacArthur IV, who has never married, is a concert pianist, writer and artist and lives in Greenwich Village, New York, under an assumed name.

FIELD MARSHAL EARL WAVELL's
'FORM OF DAILY SERVICE'

While serving as Viceroy of India between 1943 and 1947, Field Marshal Earl Wavell included in his commonplace book a 'Form of Daily Service for Use in all Departments of the Government of India':

O Lord grant us this day we come to no decisions, neither run into any kind of responsibility; but that all our doings may be so ordered as to establish new and quite unwarranted Departments, for ever and ever …

THE FAR EAST
PRISONERS OF WAR (FEPOW) PRAYER

Corporal Arthur Ogden of the 1st Battalion, The Leicestershire Regiment, and Victor Merrett of the Hong Kong Dockyard Defence Corps collaborated on this prayer, on display in the FEPOW Memorial Building at the National Memorial Arboretum at Alrewas in Staffordshire:

And we that are left grow old with the years,
  Remembering the heartache, the pain and the tears;
Hoping and praying that never again
  Man will sink to such sorrow and shame.
The price that was paid we will always remember
  Every day, every month, not just in November.

'ABSENT VETERANS'
THE KOREAN WAR 1950-3

On the morning of 22 April 1951 Padre 'Sam' Davies con-
ducted a service of Holy Communion for the officers and
men of the 1st Battalion, The Gloucestershire Regiment, who
were soon to be attacked in overwhelming strength by the
Chinese on the line of the Imjin River. Three days later, the
'Glorious Glosters' were surrounded on a feature later renamed
Gloucester Hill and, realising where his duty lay, Davies surrendered, remarking: 'This looks like a holiday in Peking for
some of us.' There followed a 600-mile march, mostly by night
in order to avoid UN air surveillance, to the officers' prisoner-
of-war camp, known as Camp 2.

The prisoners hoarded rice paper, on which was later written a copy of the Book of Common Prayer. That first Christmas,
the Chinese gave Padre 'Sam' Davies a loaf of bread and a
bottle of wine so that he could celebrate Holy Communion;
however, this was exceptional and was only permitted on four
more occasions during the remaining two years of captivity.
As a prisoner of officer status, Davies was not allowed to go
amongst the other ranks. Padre 'Sam' Davies always ended his
services with the first two lines of a hymn written in 1849 by
Frederick William Faber in memory of the Catholic martyrs of
the English Reformation:

Faith of our fathers, living still,
In spite of dungeon, fire and sword.

I was privileged to represent The Not Forgotten Association
at a Service of Thanksgiving in Westminster Abbey on 11 July

2013 to celebrate the sixtieth anniversary of the cessation of hostilities in the Korean War. During the service, 'Absent Veterans' – written by Private David Lidstone, The Gloucestershire Regiment, who died in 2004 – was read:

Would that you could wander still
  Through grassy fields, by wooded hill
When morning birds-song fills the air
  And yet another spring is here.

If only you could still feel the sun
  Upon your face when winter's done,
And smell sweet-scented flowers fair
  When yet another summer's here.

But Fate decided otherwise
  And you, beneath Korean skies,
A gallant band of comrades lie,
  Your duty done, your merit high.

No changing seasons can erase
  That once familiar name, that face
Which comes and lingers in each thought
  Of those with whom we lived and fought.

Things to Remember

During a school speech day after the First World War, the former Chief of the Imperial General Staff, Field Marshal Sir William 'Wully' Robertson, said:

> *Boys, I have a great deal to say to you but it won't take long, so remember it:*[1]
>
> *1. Speak the truth.*
> *2. Think of others.*
> *3. Don't dawdle.*

In 1956, the diplomat, archaeologist and historian, Stewart Perowne, perhaps best known for his brief *mariage blanc* with explorer and travel writer, Freya Stark, proffered four rules of politics in the Middle East, where the British Armed Services have recently garnered a great deal of experience:

> *1. Always keep the initiative.*
> *2. Always exploit the inevitable.*
> *3. Always keep in with the 'outs'.*
> *4. Never stand between a dog and a lamp-post.*

Eric Fletcher was a miner's son who matriculated at King's College, Cambridge in 1945 and served as an Education

---

[1] John G. Murray, *A Gentleman Publisher's Commonplace Book*, London: John Murray, 1996.

Officer in the Royal Air Force 1948–50. His advice to members of the Armed Services was:[2]

1. Keep a copy.
2. Pass the buck.
3. Volunteer for fuck all.

According to an old saying, cited by Norman Dixon, young soldiers were offered some solid advice during basic training:

1. If it moves, salute it.
2. If it doesn't, pick it up.
3. If you can't, paint it.

Strange though this may seem, it is not so very far from the truth: alternate kerbstones outside the guardroom of the 1st Battalion, The Devonshire and Dorset Regiment were painted grass green and tawny orange, reflecting the regiment's colours.

On 12 October 1974, less than a week after I had gone up to university, my father, who was Colonel of the Regiment when I was commissioned, wrote:

I am not a great one for giving advice but there are three things which you might remember. They are:

1. Live within your means – thrift has many rewards (and this I think you have already learned).

---

[2] E. M. Forster, *Commonplace Book*, ed. Philip Gardner, London: Scolar Press, 1988, p. 195.

2. Relax! Don't even try smoking and confine your drinking to wine and beer. Tobacco and spirits are bad for blood pressure.
3. Work hard – the results of your degree will stay with you the whole of your life.

On 10 February 1991, Major (now Major General Sir) Sebastian Roberts, Irish Guards, produced a slightly tongue-in-cheek cartoon entitled 'Rules for Guards Officers' in which he advised that, when in London, never:

1. Abbreviate.
2. Hail a taximeter cabriolet.
3. Use public transport.
4. Unfurl an umbrella.
5. Carry a parcel (bigger than 1″×2″×3″).
6. Wear a brigade tie,
7. Especially with a boating jacket,
8. Or, most especially, blue denim trousers.

POSTSCRIPT

The thing that I remember most clearly is the wonderful way that soldiers had with words. In the late summer of 1978, I was in command of my platoon during Exercise Medicine Man 4, which took place near Suffield in Alberta, in the heart of the Canadian prairie. Every tree – and there were only half a dozen of them in more than a thousand square miles – was marked on the map. After a quick inspection of the ground, I asked the men, 'Well, what do you think?' One of them piped up: 'Well, Sir, this is what you call wall-to-wall fuck-all, Sir.'

Bibliography

Hints, Subalterns, for Use of, Leicester: C. H. Gee & Co. Ltd., 1943.

Instructions for American Servicemen in Britain 1942, Oxford: Bodleian Library, 2004.

Instructions for British Servicemen in France 1944, Oxford: Bodleian Library, 2005.

Brewer's Dictionary of Phrase & Fable, Millennium Edition, London: Cassell Publishers Ltd., 1999.

Irish Guards: Notes for Officers, London, 2013.

Brittain, Vera, *Testament of Youth,* London: Victor Gollancz, 1933.

Broome, Jack, *Make A Signal,* London: Putnam, 1955.

Broome, Jack, *Make Another Signal,* London: William Kimber & Co. Ltd., 1973.

Bush, Eric, *Salute the Soldier,* London: George Allen & Unwin Ltd., 1966.

Carew, Tim, *How the Regiments Got Their Nicknames,* Barnsley: Leo Cooper, 1975.

Dixon, Norman, *On the Psychology of Military Incompetence,* London: Jonathan Cape, 1976.

Edwards, Adam, *A Short History of the Wellington Boot,* London: Hodder & Stoughton, 2006.

Forster, Edward Morgan, *Commonplace Book,* ed. Philip Gardner, London: Scolar Press, 1988.

Grose, Francis, *Advice to the Officers of the British Army with the Addition of Some Hints to the Drummer and Soldier,* London: Jonathan Cape, 1946.

Holmes, Richard, *Redcoat: The British Soldier in the Age of Horse and Musket,* London: HarperCollins, 2001.

Holmes, Richard, *Sahib: The British Soldier in India,* London: HarperPress, 2005.

Holmes, Richard, *Soldiers: A Social History*, London: HarperPress, 2012.

Murray, John G., *A Gentleman Publisher's Commonplace Book*, London: John Murray, 1996.

Mussell, John W., ed., *The Token Book of Militarisms: A Compendium of Abbreviations, Synonyms, Acronyms and Slangwords as Used by the Armed Forces of the World*, Axminster: Token Publishing, 1995.

Norwich, John Julius, 2nd Viscount, *A Christmas Cracker: Being a Commonplace Selection*, (various), privately published.

The Oxford Dictionary of Quotations, Second Edition, Oxford: Oxford University Press, 1978.

Rutter, Owen, ed., *We Happy Few*, London: Golden Cockerel Press, 1946.

Sellar, Walter Carruthers and Yeatman, Robert Julian, *1066 And All That*, London: Methuen & Co., 1930.

Shewell-Cooper, Wilfred, *Land Girl: A Manual for Volunteers in the Women's Land Army 1941*, London: English Universities Press, 1941.

Stanhope, Philip Henry, *Notes on Conversations with the Duke of Wellington*, London: privately published, 1886.

Swinton, Ernest Dunlop, *The Defence of Duffer's Drift*, London: William Clowes, 1904.

Taylor, Stephen, *Commander: The Life and Exploits of Britain's Greatest Frigate Captain*, London: Faber and Faber Ltd., 2012.

Vernède, Robert Ernest, *War Poems and Other Verses*, London: William Heinemann, 1917.

Wavell, Archibald Percival, 1st Earl, *Notes and Ideas 1939–46*, privately published.

Wesley, John, *A Word in Season, or, Advice to a Soldier*, Newcastle-upon-Tyne: J. Gooding, 1744.

Wolseley, Garnet, *The Soldier's Pocket-Book for Field Service*, London: Macmillan & Co., 1869.

www.armedforces.co.uk

www.arrse.co.uk

Acknowledgements

I am extremely grateful for the help that I have received from many people, including John Bendit, James Bryant, Lord Dannatt, David Day, Andrew Freemantle, Toby Glover, David Harrison, the late Richard Holmes, William Hurrell, Lucy Kellaway, Harry McGowan, Ron MacKenzie, Patrick Mercer, Bill Mott, Geoff Nicholls, Robert Osborn, Chey Palacios, Sir Michael Parker, Tim Purdon, Robert Raffety, Sebastian Roberts, John Saumarez Smith, Derek Smyth, Stephen Taylor, Robbie Wilmont, Ashe Windham and Henry Worsley, as well as the support that I have had from my wife, Amanda.

There are two people, though, who have made an invaluable contribution to *A Military Miscellany*: Matilda Hunt, whose charming illustrations inject variety and bring different aspects of the book to life; and my old friend, Peter Wall, who somehow found time in his extraordinarily busy schedule to read the book, before pinpointing – in very few words – exactly what I am trying to achieve.

Once again, I acknowledge my debt to the very supportive team at Elliott & Thompson, without whom *A Military Miscellany* would never have been brought to fruition: Lorne Forsyth, Olivia Bays, Pippa Crane, Carol Anderson and Alison Menzies.

Index